Advance praise for
Ornament of Dakpo Kagyü Thought

"Everybody in the Kagyü lineage knows the pithy and touching verses of the third Karmapa's famous *Aspiration Prayer of Mahāmudrā*, which are like the well-shaped limbs of a beautiful body. Their being adorned by Mendong Tsampa's concise *Ornament* skillfully elicits just the right amount of thoughts to shine a light on thought-free mahāmudrā. In the mirror of Sarah Harding's fine introduction and translation, we are now enabled to clearly see all these adornments pointing back at naked mahāmudrā in its unadorned state."

—Karl Brunnhölzl, author of *Milarepa's Kungfu: Mahāmudrā in His Songs of Realization*

"I well remember, during our three-year retreat, when I shared with Sarah this delightful commentary on the third Karmapa's *Mahāmudrā Aspiration Prayer*. The pleasure and benefit I derived at that time from reading Mendong Tsampa's words are mirrored now by the pleasure of knowing that Sarah has brought this gem into English for others to benefit."

—Richard Barron (Chökyi Nyima), translator of *The Autobiography of Jamgön Kongtrul: A Gem of Many Colors*

"Sarah Harding clarifies the essence of mahāmudrā with characteristic humor and penetrating insight, including points of contention. These pithy texts, elegantly translated, are contemplations on lucid awareness and immeasurable compassion, sparking illumination while refreshing one's language skills!"

—Karma Lekshe Tsomo, professor of Buddhist Studies, University of San Diego

"Mendong Tsampa's commentary on the third Karmapa's famous *Mahāmudrā Aspiration Prayer* is a perfect balance of depth and concision, and Sarah Harding's presentation—from her introduction to her translation and notes—also strikes the perfect balance of precision and readability. *Ornament of Dakpo Kagyü Thought* opens up the profundity and brilliance of the *Mahāmudrā Aspiration Prayer* in a direct and lucid way—it's the middle-length commentary we've all needed! This book will be savored by all who are inspired by the path of mahāmudrā, from those starting out to seasoned Buddhist practitioners and scholars."

—Elizabeth Callahan, translator of *Moonbeams of Mahāmudrā*

Ornament of
Dakpo Kagyü Thought

SHORT COMMENTARY ON THE
Mahāmudrā Aspiration Prayer

BY MENDONG TSAMPA,
KARMA NGEDÖN TENGYÉ

*Translated, introduced, and annotated
by Sarah Harding*

Wisdom Publications
199 Elm Street
Somerville, MA 02144 USA
wisdomexperience.org

Library of Congress Cataloging-in-Publication Data
Names: Karma-nges-don-bstan-rgyas, active 1891, author. | Harding, Sarah,
    1951– translator.
Title: Ornament of Dakpo Kagyü thought: short commentary on the
    Mahāmudrā aspiration prayer / by Mendong Tsampa Karma Ngedön Tengyé;
    translated, introduced, and annotated by Sarah Harding.
Description: First edition. | Somerville: Wisdom Publications, 2022. |
    Includes bibliographical references and index.
Identifiers: LCCN 2021056664 (print) | LCCN 2021056665 (ebook) |
    ISBN 9781614297185 (paperback) | ISBN 9781614297314 (ebook)
Subjects: LCSH: Mahāmudrā (Tantric rite). | Bka'-brgyud-pa (Sect)—Rituals. |
    Buddhist poetry, Tibetan—History and criticism.
Classification: LCC BQ8921.M35 2022 (print) | LCC BQ8921.M35 (ebook) |
    DDC 294.3/4435—dc23/eng/20220202
LC record available at https://lccn.loc.gov/2021056664
LC ebook record available at https://lccn.loc.gov/2021056665

ISBN 978-1-61429-718-5   ebook ISBN 978-1-61429-731-4

26 25 24 23 22   5 4 3 2 1

Cover design by Gopa & Ted 2. Interior design by Tony Lulek.
Cover image: An ancient seal of the Karmapas, used with permission of His Holiness Ogyen Trinley Dorje, the Seventeenth Karmapa.

Printed on acid-free paper that meets the guidelines for permanence and durability of the Production Guidelines for Book Longevity of the Council on Library Resources.

Printed in the United States of America.

MIX
Paper from
responsible sources
FSC® C011935

Please visit fscus.org.

Contents

Preface

The *Aspiration Prayer of Definitive Mahāmudrā* by Lord Rangjung Dorjé has long been my favorite prayer, ever since its daily recitation as part of the curriculum in the three-year retreat. It seems to just roll off the tongue (in Tibetan, that is), yet without losing transparency of meaning like many other lightning-fast recitations. I have used many of its verses in Tibetan classes over the years, particularly for exercises in memorization, as well as translation. In the two-week summer Tibetan Intensive of 2018, sponsored by the Tsadra Foundation and held at the University of Colorado Boulder, I decided to use this lovely and accessible commentary by Mendong Tsampa Rinpoché as the study topic for the advanced track in classical Tibetan. It was a remarkable experience to work on this as a group, and an intelligent group at that. I am used to working alone, but this was a very enriching process for me, and hopefully for the students as well. There was so much interchange of ideas and words and research, I really regard it as an international committee translation project, although admittedly I had the last say in this final translation submitted to Wisdom Publications. I would therefore like to mention and thank all of the students. I am sure many of them will go on to be well-known scholar-practitioners (if they are not already).

Alina Cepeda
Ralph H. Craig III
Allan Yi Ding
Renée Ford
Tucker Foley
Benjamin Goldstein
Cheryl Lins
Aaron McNeil
Katrin Querl

Our support team from the Tsadra Foundation, Marcus Perman and the staff, facilitated the ease of learning, and our ever-helpful Tibetan informant, Ācārya Lama Tenpa Gyaltsen, clarified difficult points. Many of these students were also in Jules Levinson's advanced colloquial class, where they listened to tapes of Khenchen Thrangu Rinpoché's teachings on the same prayer, which must now be indelibly etched in their minds forever, as it is in mine. Of course we could not finish the whole translation in two weeks, but I kept plugging away at it to the end with two hardy and highly motivated students: Tucker Foley and Ben Goldstein.

And so I present this final product in the hopes that ever more students and their teachers will find it useful—for inspiration, for studying Tibetan, for the awakening of the world.

Sarah Harding
Boulder, Colorado
August 2021

INTRODUCTION

The *Mahāmudrā Aspiration Prayer* by the Third Karmapa Rangjung Dorjé (1284–1339) is certainly one of the most brilliant and popular compositions we have on mahāmudrā. What seems to be a heartfelt prayer in twenty-five quatrains of easygoing nine-meter verse that lends itself to chanting and ritualized group prayer is at the same time intricately organized into the most profound and thorough exposition of the practice and theory of mahāmudrā, the pinnacle of practice in the Kagyü school of Buddhism in Tibet. Because of that, it is widely used even now, some seven centuries later, both as a deep contemplative practice and as a springboard for far-ranging Dharma talks.

The earliest written commentary appeared about four centuries later (in 1733), composed by the great lineage holder Situ Paṇchen Chökyi Jungné, Tenpai Nyinjé (1700–1774). *The Oral Transmission of the Supreme Siddhas*, though described by its author as "brief," is a good example of how the great masters and erudites of Tibet could expand a short prayer into an encyclopedia of Buddhist thought. A lot to handle for the average meditator. Mendong Tsampa Rinpoché (1867–1921?), exercising kindness to the reader, composed this *Ornament of Dakpo Kagyü Thought*, reducing it by about one-third. His contemporary, Karma Rinchen Dargyé (ca. 1835–ca. 1917), made an even shorter version.[1] But as Goldilocks discovered, the middle way is perfect.

MAHĀMUDRĀ

Mahāmudrā as we know it is a name for the practice and culminating realization of nondual suchness in several lineages of Tibetan Buddhism, especially in the Kagyü. However, the term itself, as well as the practice, had a long and somewhat complicated history along a bumpy road before it arrived at this pristine state. The simplest level of complication is twofold: that it means one thing in a tantric context and another in relation to sutra or the path of the perfections. But even in that there is much to unpack. Fortunately for us, and especially for someone writing a bare-bones introduction, there are now many studies and publications to do that.

In Sanskrit, *mahā* means "great" or "big," and that's where the simplicity ends. The root meaning of the term *mudrā* is "seal," and by extension the imprints left by a seal, like signs or symbols.[2] In Indian literature it further indicates a ritual hand gesture or pose (from the Indian traditions of dance), a yogic posture, and the consort of a male practitioner or deity. In connection with the first meaning, we often see the English translation "great seal" with concordant explanations. The Tibetan translators added an honorific "hand" (*phyag*) to seal (*rgya*), making "chakgya chenpo" (*phyag rgya chen po*). Although there is no "hand" in the Sanskrit, that didn't stop Tibetan commentators from engaging in one of their favorite scholarly activities, often called "creative etymology." For example:

> *Hand* is the timeless awareness of emptiness.
> *Seal* means that there is nothing beyond that.
> *Great* means there is nothing higher than that.[3]

Traditionally mahāmudrā is described as that which seals all phenomena, like a sovereign's sealed edict, such that once that true nature is realized, there is nothing to which it does not apply—it is the law of the land. Here is a similar example from Situ Tenpai Nyinjé's commentary:

> The essence of mahāmudrā is untransgressable (*mi 'da'*), so mahāmudrā is called a "seal" (*mudrā; phyag rgya*). For example, just as local ministers, governors, and so on cannot transgress the command that has the seal of authority of a great universal sovereign, in the same way, the variety of inner and outer phenomena do not transgress the essence of unified spontaneous timeless awareness. That is why it is a seal. *Mahā* means it is great, because it is the essence of the three [other seals]: action seal, dharma seal, and pledge seal.[4]

There are many more such profound explanations. Generally, though, they do not take into account the full range of meanings for *mudrā*, which carry over to *mahāmudrā*.

In the context of the tantras, mahāmudrā is often part of a set of the four mudrās mentioned above: action seal (*karmamudrā*), dharma seal (*dharmamudrā*), pledge seal (*samayamudrā*), and great seal (*mahāmudrā*). A certain succession developed to these four in terms of progressive realization, and they are related to the four empowerments in a highest yoga tantra initiation. Some recent scholarship on ancient Dunhuang manuscripts suggests that it wasn't always this order, that samayamudrā and mahāmudrā were reversed, with mahāmudrā referring only to the complete form of the deity.[5] Be that as it may, there is a long tradition of the progressive understanding in both Indian and Tibetan literature that emphasizes mahāmudrā as the ultimate realization of mind's nature, which is arrived at after experiencing the other mudrā practices in the context of a tantric initiation. Mudrā can also refer to a spiritual partner or consort, either real or imagined, depending on the stage of the initiation, union with whom leads to various experiences of bliss. Mahāmudrā, then, is only realized in the fourth and last empowerment, when the mahāmudrā consort is a spontaneous reflection of one's own mind and the ultimate union of bliss and emptiness is realized.

The highest yoga tantras where these teachings were primarily expounded arrived from India into Tibet during the second wave of Buddhist transmission and quickly became established. At the same time, esoteric instructions based on the tantras passed in person from living Indian masters to Tibetans, either in India itself or in Tibet. This exchange was the breeding ground for all the "new" (*gsar ma*) schools of Buddhism in Tibet, after which everything from the earlier spread was labeled as "ancient" (*snying ma*).

THE KAGYÜ TREATMENT OF MAHĀMUDRĀ

The Kagyü school traces its Tibetan lineage to Marpa Chökyi Lodrö (ca. 1010–ca. 1090), who traveled to India and received teachings from extraordinary adepts, most notably Nāropa and Maitrīpa. Nāropa had received tantric transmissions from Tilopa, which were later formalized in a set of practices familiar as the Six Dharmas of Nāropa. The teachings that Marpa received from Maitrīpa, who had received them from the master Śavaripa, were mainly non-tantric instructions based on a practice of letting the mind settle in its own state, or mental nonengagement (*yid la mi byed pa*), that was being disseminated by the Indian mahāsiddhas. Of special note in this tradition was Saraha, whose teachings came to Tibet through the medium of dohās, a form of poetic composition in rhyming couplets, and other compositions.[6] Saraha is therefore considered the forefather of the Kagyü mahāmudrā practice that is mostly familiar now.

Marpa Lōtsawa brought back both sets of instructions and passed them to his disciples, notably the famous Milarepa, who in turn passed them on to Rechungpa and Gampopa. It was Gampopa Sönam Rinchen (1079–1153) who established monastic centers and incorporated these teachings with those of Atiśa's Kadampa lineage, which was mainly based on sutras and the gradual path, or *lam rim*. Gampopa gathered many disciples, some of them famous for being the founders of suborders, known as the four early and eight later Kagyü lineages. He also began to call the mahāsiddha teachings on mental nonengagement "mahāmudrā" and allowed his disciples to teach them around the vast country with only a consecration or authorization ritual of Vajravārāhī rather than a full fourfold tantric initiation, so that many disciples would have the opportunity to practice these essential Dharma teachings. Dakpo Tashi Namgyal (1512/13–1587), in his classic *Moonbeams of Mahāmudrā*, states:

The teachers of this meditational lineage up to Milarepa meditated mainly on the key instructions of the Mantrayāna mysticism while at various times incorporating vital instructions on mahāmudrā from the discourses on the yogas of inner heat and lucid awareness. Yet the great master Gampopa, having been moved by immeasurable compassion, expounded mainly on the quintessential instructions on mahāmudrā. As a result, it became widely known as the single path for all predestined seekers.[7]

According to Jamgön Kongtrul, Gampopa continued to teach the tantric path of Nāropa's Six Dharmas as well as this "new" mahāmudrā that he says derived from the Kadampa lineage:

[Gampopa] taught his regular disciples the Kadampa stages of the path and the meditative absorption from the tradition that is adorned with the name *mahāmudrā*. He taught the uncommon mahāmudrā of Mantra connected to Lama Mila's path of skillful methods to his extraordinary disciples.[8]

The essence of this mahāmudrā is very close indeed to that in the myriad sutras on the perfection of wisdom (*prajñāpāramitā*), so it eventually became known as "sutra mahāmudrā," as distinguished from the tantric mahāmudrā mentioned above. It became "adorned" (as in Kongtrul's careful word choice) by elements of a progressive path, with the practices of calm abiding and higher insight as the foundation of the journey that leads through four stages of realization, known as the four yogas: one-pointedness, freedom from elaboration, single flavor, and nonmeditation. And thus it remains to the present day.

But back then, the brilliant if slightly puritanical scholar Sakya Paṇḍita Kunga Gyaltsen (1182–1251) was not at all happy with this development. The rebuttal that took aim directly at Gampopa and the Kagyü schools came in his famous text, *A Clear Differentiation of the Three Codes*, written around 1232.[9] This is a scathing assessment of the state of Buddhism, and particularly Vajrayāna in Tibet, barely disguised as a discussion of the three levels of vows. Sakya Paṇḍita's motivation was certainly to differentiate and separate those systems and to point out incidents and indiscretions of crossing over, inaccuracy, hybridity, and misapplication. But the polemic goes far beyond just that, and with his searing logic he calls into question many issues of lineage, appropriation, false advertising, false gurus, false empowerments, and everything else false about, particularly, the Kagyü. The gist of it was simple, as reported by Jamgön Kongtrul:

> Mahāmudrā is not designated in the tradition
> of the perfections. The pristine awareness of
> mahāmudrā only arises from empowerment.[10]

The response to this attack was...silence...for a few centuries, while it soaked in.[11] But by the fifteenth century the Kagyü defense was in full swing, responding to Sakya Paṇḍita's accusations and those of his later followers, such as Gorampa Sönam Sengé (1429–63).[12] The debate raged on, and seems to show up in almost all the Kagyü commentaries of the time. There are very good and interesting points to be made, and it is both rewarding and fun to investigate these issues.

Having done that, to save you time, my conclusion is that Gampopa prevails in the end.[13] Why? Simply by virtue of the renown and popularity of "his" mahāmudrā, the so-called sutra and essence mahāmudrā that eclipsed all other versions in the popular mind and is now simply *the* mahāmudrā. And it is arguably the most useful. Not only that, it is clear that its authentic source is the tradition of Indian mahāsiddhas that is replete with such teachings, which both Tibetan scholars and academics have repeatedly demonstrated. Klaus-Dieter Mathes concludes:

> It should be noted that sūtra-based mahāmudrā teachings have Indian roots which can be clearly identified. To sum up, the blending of the Sūtras with the Tantras is something that definitely started in India and not in Tibet.[14]

And as the great Padma Karpo (1527–92) said, "Worrying about the reasons for [the Kagyüs] having it or not is like [worrying about] whether a rabbit's horns are sharp or dull." He confessed to being worn out by the whole thing.[15]

This mahāmudrā that reveals the true nature of one's own mind and thence that of all phenomena has been preeminent in all Kagyü lineages since then, along with the yogic teachings from Nāropa. One of the great disciples of Gampopa and Rechungpa was Düsum Khyenpa (1110–93). He became retroactively the first in a series of recognized reincarnations, the Karmapas, which is thought of as the earliest case of the now ubiquitous tulku system of incarnate lamas. Düsum Khyenpa also marks the beginning of the Karma Kagyü suborder, also known as Kamtsang Kagyü. The second Karmapa, Karma Pakshi (1204–83), inherited the monasteries and authority of his predecessor.[16] The third Karmapa was Rangjung Dorjé (1284–1339), the author of the *Aspiration Prayer of Definitive Mahāmudrā*.

KARMAPA RANGJUNG DORJÉ

With all the schools and subschools, it might seem to be very systematic with everyone keeping in their own lane. In fact these early masters received and practiced instructions from many sources. Karmapa Rangjung Dorjé exemplifies this well. He composed widely on a variety of topics and is considered a preeminent figure not only in the Kagyü lineages but also those of Severance, or Chö (*gcod*), and Nyingma. He composed treatises that became the foundation for studies by generations of meditators and scholars in the Karma Kagyü tradition and beyond, ranging from the massive commentary on the highest yoga tantras, *The Profound Inner Principles* (*Zab mo nang don*), to condensed profound supplications such as the *Aspiration Prayer of Mahāmudrā*. Though this last stands on its own as a deep contemplative practice, it took a later Kagyü tulku, the great Situ Pema Nyinjé Chökyi Jungné, to unlock all that it contains in his commentary, *The Oral Transmission of the Supreme Siddhas*. This commentary is not only instructive, but the reverence that the author demonstrates for his ancestral Karmapa is abundantly evident and heartwarming. Mendong Tsampa Rinpoché likewise displays the same devotional attitude, one that has not diminished at all with the years but seems to grow with each successive generation. Further commentary on these commentaries would be wholly redundant, but it is hoped the respect and devotion will continue to manifest in you, the readers.

MENDONG TSAMPA RINPOCHÉ

Mendong Tsampa is an interesting character and almost our contemporary. I'm sure that many of the beloved Kagyü masters that my generation has been fortunate to meet must have met him or his students. One of those was the late Bokar Rinpoché, Karma Ngedön Chökyi Lodrö (1940–2004), the successor too briefly of Khyabjé Kalu Rinpoché in the Shangpa lineage. The Mendong and Bokar monasteries are close by each other in Tshochen (Coqen) county, Ngari prefecture, in western Tibet. It was Bokar Rinpoché who organized the printing of the three-volume collection of Mendong Tsampa's works. The following is a loose translation of the brief life story that Bokar Rinpoché included at the end of the third volume.

Lamp for the Minds of the Faithful: A Rough Sketch of the Activities of the Glorious Guru[17]
by Bokar Tulku Rinpoché

> Your smiling face of all victors' compassion, like camphor
>   pollen,
> emanates in a single drop the signs and marks of the
>   awakened,
> ensuring the benefit and well-being of all great secret
>   tantras:
> I bow to the guru, skilled in inviting the four kāya guests.

Tsampa Rinpoché of Mendong Monastery in Tö (Gtod) was named Karma Ngedön Tengyé Mawai Sengé Palzangpo. In the upper snow ranges near Mount Tisé (Kailash), which was prophesied by the Victor as the celestial palace of Cakrasaṃvara in the mandala of the ḍākinīs of the three sacred sites, there is one of the nine tribes called Drongmé ('Brong smad). In the northeast of Drong, in the confluence of the vast valley, in a town called Makyayu (Ma skya yu) in the precious landscape, he was born in the year 1867 of the Western calendar; the earth female rabbit year of the fifteenth cycle. His stepfather was Trapun and his mother Josang Chödrön. After he was conceived, his mother dreamed of light radiating from her navel and filling all the land with light. Her body felt light and healthy, and many good omens occurred. After only seven months he was born amidst rainbows and brilliant lights appearing in the clear sky. He was given the name Jamyang Palden. While still young, he trained in letters and learned how to read and write. As he grew up, he naturally had a great affinity for the Dharma and had no desire to pursue this world. However, his parents, in accord with the general customs, invited a girl called Akar to be his bride. At twenty-five he had become very knowledgeable, so at the villagers' request he built a dwelling in the town. Like the father of a hundred children, he was always fair to everyone and became worthy of everyone's respect.

On one occasion, while traveling to the south, his horse was stolen and he decided to pursue the matter. The local minster held a trial, but the magistrate was biased in favor of the thief, so Rinpoché became very sad. He took the case to the central government in Lhasa to file a lawsuit. As a form of collateral, he offered horses and mules. The court came to a verdict about the thief and they called for the local magistrate. Rinpoché's representative waited for the result in Lhasa. But that biased judge who had made his decision even before the trial was too ashamed to show up in court. So Rinpoché forfeited his horses and mules and went to Tsurphu Monastery [the main seat of the Karmapas].

At Tsurphu he met the fifteenth Gyalwang Karmapa, Khakhyab Dorjé (1870/71–1921/22), and gradually took the levels of monastic ordination. He studied sutras, tantras, and classical texts with many experts. He met the refuge lord Chöwang Tulku Rinpoché and received all the empowerments and instructions on the profound meaning of the great Secret Mantra Vehicle, like pouring all the contents from one pot into another. He became a master of all areas of knowledge. Through complete mastery of the paths of methods and liberation, he could control his own wind-mind. He became totally free of stains of the eight worldly concerns, or any kind of pretense. He kept silent for many years and sealed off his retreat place, passing the time in that way. He blazed in glory through his powers of knowledge and love. By speaking spontaneously he became a great orator.

He thought he should do something for the people, so he came back to the upper valley. By then he had become sick with gout, so he had to travel by yak wherever he was invited. After returning home, he spent time only in recitation retreat in a one-person tent. Life and practice had became identical. Between sessions, to fulfill students' wishes, he gave empowerments, guidance, and wrote commentaries on the treatises and oral instructions, creating a vast and profound body of work. He performed a special consecration in the beautiful

Vajra Court of the Bodhi Medicine Tree, the gathering place of the sangha.

The gout caused his legs to swell, but he would not treat it, so the swelling burst open to the point where the bones were visible. The area became infected and odorous, oozing dark pus. Rather than cleaning it, he took an oath of generosity to let bugs and maggots consume the rotting flesh. His lower body became all bony. To demonstrate impermanence, Mendong Tsampa Rinpoché passed away in the iron bird year (1921) at the age of eighty-two. The Karmapa gave the order not to cremate his body, but rather to enshrine it in a stupa with the face showing, as a seed of fortune for future disciples. Known as a special sublime support, it became famous as an object of liberation upon seeing.

He had many students, including his younger brother Khenchen Lungrik Gyaltsen, who became a great master. When he passed away, he was cremated and his ashes were divided between Mendong and Bokar Monasteries. The two younger sisters, the elder Kunzang Drolma and the younger Karma Chönyi, were also great practitioners. The latter passed away at ninety-four in a water horse year (1942) with her body shrunken to one cubit in length. Other students were Ane Chödzé Rinpoché, Drupön Sherab Thogmé, Drupön Karma Tsewang, Lhajé Yeshé Gyaltsen, Drupön Adamchö Rinpoché, Karma Döndam Gyurmé, and the amazing Lama Rapga Rinpoché.

This story was gathered from the oral accounts of scholars and ordinary old people who knew him. As firsthand accounts, nothing was made up or omitted. However, his commentaries and oral instructions were never before gathered in one place and had remained scattered. Apart from that, if other scholars know more information on his amazing activities, including other information on dates, then they can add to this short account, which was written for the printing of his *Collected Works*.

Aspiration Prayer of Definitive Mahāmudrā

by Karmapa Rangjung Dorjé

Namo guru

1. Gurus and yidams, deities of the mandala,
victors of the ten directions and three times, and heirs,
consider me with love and bless me so my aspirations
will be accomplished just as intended.

2. A stream of virtues not muddied by the three spheres
descends the snow mountain of totally pure thoughts and
    deeds,
mine and those of infinite sentient beings;
may it flow into the ocean of the victors' four kāyas.

3. Until that comes to pass, however long it takes,
throughout life after life in the future,
with even the sounds "sin" and "suffering" unknown;
may I enjoy the glorious sea of happiness and virtue.

4. Free and endowed; having faith, vigor, and wisdom,
attending a good spiritual master, receiving the nectar of
   teachings,
and properly practicing them without obstacles;
may I engage in the holy Dharma in all future lifetimes.

5. Studying scripture and logic liberates from obscurations of
   unknowing.
Contemplating esoteric instruction vanquishes doubt's
   darkness.
Light from meditation illuminates the abiding nature as it is.
May the brilliance of these three wisdoms increase.

6. "Ground" means the two truths free of extreme eternalism
   or nihilism.
"Supreme path" is two accumulations free of extreme impo-
   sition or denial.
This leads to the result: the two benefits free of extreme
   existence or peace.
May I meet the Dharma without deviation or error.

7. The ground of refining is mind itself, the unity of
   clarity-emptiness.
The refiner is the great vajra yoga of mahāmudrā.
It refines the object, the stains of incidental delusion.
May I actualize the refined result, stainless dharmakāya.

8. Deep confidence in the view is to sever impositions on the
   ground.
The vital point of meditation is to hold that without
   distraction.

Best conduct is to exercise skill in all meanings of
    meditation.
May I have deep confidence in view, meditation, and
    conduct.

9. All phenomena are projections of the mind.
As for mind, there is no mind—it is empty of an essence.
But, while empty, it appears freely as anything at all.
Examining this thoroughly, may I sever its base and roots.

10. Mind's displays that never existed are mistaken for
    objects.
Innate awareness is ignorantly mistaken for a self.
We wander in the expanse of existence by such dualism.
May I get to the bottom of delusional mistakes.

11. It does not exist; even the victors don't see it.
It doesn't not exist; it's the basis of all samsara and nirvana.
No contradiction; it's the middle way of unity.
May I realize mind's true nature without extremes.

12. To say "this is" doesn't indicate anything.
To say "this is not" doesn't refute anything.
Unformed true nature defies the intellect.
May I gain certainty in the range of genuine reality.

13. Not to realize this is to flounder in samsara's ocean.
To realize it is nothing other than buddhahood.
Being all, "this is it" and "this is not it" mean nothing at all.
May I awaken to the true nature hidden in the all-ground.

14. As appearance is mind, so too emptiness is mind.
As realization is mind, delusion is also one's mind.
As birth is mind, so is cessation the mind.
May I sever all the impositions of mind.

15. Unspoiled by meditation with mind-made effort,
unmoved by the winds of everyday affairs,
knowing how to fall naturally in the uncontrived innate state;
may I skillfully maintain the practice of mind's meaning.

16. The waves of subtle and coarse thoughts subside in
     themselves.
The river of unmoved mind abides within itself.
Free of the murky stains of dullness and darkness,
may the unmoving ocean of calm abiding be steady.

17. When you look again and again for imperceptible mind,
you see distinctly the meaning of not seeing, just as it is.
Severing doubts about the meaning of being and nonbeing,
may I know my own unmistakable nature.

18. When you look at objects, there are no objects, you see
     mind.
Looking at mind, there is no mind; empty of essence.
Looking at both frees dualistic fixation in its own place.
May I realize lucid clarity, the abiding nature of mind.

19. Free of mental engagement; this is mahāmudrā.
Free of extremes; this is mahāmadhyamaka.
All-inclusive, it is also called mahāsandhi.
May I gain confidence that knowing one is realizing all.

20. The great bliss free of attachment is continuous.
Lucid clarity without fixation on attributes is free of obscuring veils.
Nonthought beyond intellect is spontaneously present.
May these experiences occur continuously without effort.

21. Attachment fixated on good experience subsides on its own.
Delusion of bad thought is naturally pure in basic space.
Ordinary mind is free of acceptance and rejection, loss and gain.
May I realize the truth of unembellished true reality.

22. Though the nature of migrators is ever buddha,
they fail to realize it and wander endlessly in samsara.
May unbearable compassion be born in my being
for endlessly suffering sentient beings.

23. Unimpeded energy of unbearable compassion is love,
the meaning of its empty essence exposed.
This supreme path of unity that never deviates;
may I meditate on this day and night without interruption.

24. With the eyes and clairvoyances produced by potent meditation,
sentient beings are matured and buddha fields refined.
Aspirations for accomplishing buddha qualities are fulfilled.
May I become buddha, the ultimate fulfillment, maturation, and refinement.

25. By the compassion of the ten-direction victors and their
    heirs,
and the power of whatever pure virtue there is,
may my pure aspirations and those of all beings
all be fulfilled just as intended.

The Aspiration Prayer of Definitive Mahāmudrā *is by Lord
Rangjung Dorjé*

ORNAMENT OF DAKPO KAGYÜ THOUGHT

Short Commentary on the
Mahāmudrā Aspiration Prayer

*by Mendong Tsampa Rinpoché,
Karma Ngedön Tengyé*

ༀ། །ཕྱུག་ཆེན་སྨྲིན་ལམ་གྱི་འགྲེལ་ཆུང་དྭགས་བརྒྱུད་དགོངས་རྒྱན།

ན་མོ་གུ་རུ་མ་ཧཱ་མུ་དྲ་ཡེ། དངོས་ཀུན་ཁྱབ་བདག་དཔལ་ལྡན་རྡོ་རྗེ་
འཆང་། །དབྱེར་མེད་སྒྱོལ་བ་བཞི་ལྷུན་སྐྱམ་པོ་པ། །གང་དེའི་གསང་
གསུམ་དབང་འབྱོར་གཉྭ་ཀ །ཡབ་སྲས་བརྒྱུད་པར་བཅས་ལ་གུས།

ཕྱག་འཚལ། །དྭགས་བརྒྱུད་གྲུབ་ཐོབ་རྒྱ་མཚོ་གཤེགས་པའི་ཤུལ།
།ཟབ་ལམ་ཀུན་མཐུན་ཀུན་ལས་ཁྱད་འཕགས་པ། །ཕྱིན་ཉྭབས་རྡོ་
ལྷན་མོས་གུས་ཕྱག་ཆེན་གྱི། །སྨྲིན་ལམ་ཆིག་དོན་མདོ་ཚམ་རང་
ཉིད་ཀྱི། །དད་པའི་གསོས་སུ་དབྱེ་ལ་བྱིན་གྱིས་རློབས། །དེའང་རྒྱལ་
བའི་བསྟན་པའི་སྙིང་པོ་གདངས་ཅན་གྱི་སྟོངས་འདིར་སྒྲུབ་བརྒྱུད་
ཤིང་རྟ་ཆེན་པོ་བརྒྱུད་ཀྱི་མཆོག་རབ་མཉམ་མེད་དྭགས་པོ་བཀའ་
བརྒྱུད་ཅེས་ཡོངས་སུ་གྲགས་པ་འདི་ཉིད་ལ་ཟབ་རྒྱས་ཀྱི་ཆོས་ཚུལ་
རྒྱ་མཚོ་མཐའ་ཡས་པ་ཞིག་མཛད་བ་ལས། ཐུགས་དྭས་གྱི་གཙོ་པོ་
ཐབས་ལམ་ནཱ་རོ་ཆོས་དྲུག་དང་། གྲོལ་ལམ་ཕྱག་རྒྱ་ཆེན་པོ་གཉིས་ལ་
མཛད་པ་ལས། ཕྱི་མ་ཉིད་ཀྱི་དོན་རྣམས་ཐམས་ཅད་མཐྱིན་པ་རང་
བྱུང་ཞབས་ཀྱིས་སྨྲིན་ལམ་གྱི་ཆུལ་དུ་རྗེས་འཇུག་རྣམས་ལ་ཐུགས་
བརྩེ་བས་གདམས་པར་མཛད་པ་འདིའི་ཚིག་དོན་འོལ་སྤྱི་ཙམ་གོ་
ནའང་། མ་ཚོགས་ཚོགས་པར་བྱེད་ཅིང་། ཚོགས་པ་བོགས་དབྱུང་བའི་
གདམས་ངག་གི་གནད་བླ་མེད་དུ་གསུངས་པས། དེ་ལས་བཅད་
གསུམ། སྟོར་བ། དངོས་གཞི། རྗེས་སོ། །

Namo guru mahāmudrāya

Glorious Vajradhara, all-pervading sovereign,
inseparable from Gampopa, having four liberations,[18]
and Karmapa, master of his three secrets;
I bow in devotion to father and son with their lineage.

The road traveled by an ocean of Dakpo Kagyü adepts,
the profound path that agrees with all yet is superior to all,
possessing the blessing of warmth, is devotional mahāmudrā.
I will briefly summarize the meaning of its aspiration
so that I may receive blessings to refresh my faith.

The heart of the Victor's doctrine manifests here in the
Land of Snows as the eight great chariots of the practice lineages. Foremost among them is renowned as the incomparable Dakpo Kagyü. In this one finds an infinite ocean of
profound and vast Dharma systems. Among them, the two
principal spiritual practices that were created are the methods path of the Six Dharmas of Nāropa and the liberation
path of Mahāmudrā. Omniscient Rangjung has revealed the
meaning of the latter in the style of an aspiration prayer out of
kindness for his followers. Although we have a vague sense of
its meaning, this unsurpassed instruction in the vital points
was taught to produce new realization and enhance what has
been realized. There are three parts: preparation, main part,
and conclusion.

དང་པོ་སྟོར་བ་ནི།

ན་མོ་གུ་རུ། བླ་མ་རྣམས་དང་ཡི་དམ་དཀྱིལ་འཁོར་ལྷ། ཕྱོགས་བཅུ་
དུས་གསུམ་རྒྱལ་བ་སྲས་དང་བཅས། །བདག་ལ་བརྩེར་དགོངས་
བདག་གི་སྨོན་ལམ་རྣམས། །ཇི་བཞིན་འགྲུབ་པའི་མཐུན་འགྱུར་ཕྱིན་
རླབས་མཛོད།

།ཅིས་གསུངས་ཏེ། སྨོན་ལམ་གེགས་མེད་དུ་འགྲུབ་པའི་ཆེད་དུ་ཡུལ་
ཁྱད་པར་འཕགས་པ་རྣམས་དཔང་པོར་གསོལ་ཞིང་དེའི་དྲུང་དུ་
འདུན་པ་རྩེ་གཅིག་པས་སྨོན་ལམ་གདབ་དགོས་པར་འདོམས་པ་སྟེ།
མདོ་ལས། ཚོས་རྣམས་ཐམས་ཅད་རྐྱེན་བཞིན་དུ། །འདུན་པའི་རྩེ་ལ་
རབ་ཏུ་གནས། །གང་གིས་སྨོན་ལམ་ཅི་བཏབ་པ། །འབྲས་བུ་དེ་འདྲ་
ཁོ་ནར་སྨིན། །ཞེས་གསུངས་པས་སོ། །

གཉིས་པ་སྨོན་ལམ་དངོས་ལ། སྤྱི་དང། ཇི་བྲག གཉིས་ལས། དང་པོ་
སྤྱིར་དགེ་བ་རྫོགས་བྱང་དུ་བསྔོ་བ་ནི།

བདག་དང་མཐའ་ཡས་སེམས་ཅན་ཐམས་ཅད་ཀྱི། །བསམ་སྦྱོར་རྣམ་
དག་གདངས་རི་ལས་སྐྱེས་པའི། །འཁོར་གསུམ་རྟོག་མེད་དགེ་ཚོགས་
ཆུ་རྒྱུན་རྣམས། །རྒྱལ་བ་སྲ་བཞིའི་རྒྱ་མཚོར་འདྲུག་གྱུར་ཅིག །

I. Preparation

Namo guru

1. *Gurus and yidams, deities of the mandala,*
victors of the ten directions and three times, and heirs,
consider me with love and bless me so my aspirations
will be accomplished just as intended.

In order to **accomplish** your **aspirations** without obstruction, this prayer encourages you to solicit an especially elevated object as a witness and in their presence make your aspiration with undivided intent. It states in a sutra:

> As all phenomena are conditioned,
> they fully rest on the basis of intent.
> Whatever aspiration anyone makes,
> the fruit can only ripen accordingly.[19]

II. Main part

In the main aspiration, there are both general and particular explanations.

A. The general dedication of virtue to perfect awakening

2. *A stream of virtues not muddied by the three spheres,*
descends the snow mountain of totally pure thoughts and deeds,
mine and those of infinite sentient beings;
may it flow into the ocean of the victors' four kāyas.

ཅེས་གསུངས་ཏེ། བདག་དང་མཐའ་ཡས་པའི་སེམས་ཅན་ཐམས་ཅད་ཀྱི་དུག་གསུམ་གྱི་སེམས་དང་མ་འདྲེས་པར་བྱམས་བརྩེ་དད་མོས་སོགས་ཀྱིས་ཀུན་ནས་བསླངས་པས་བསམ་པ་རྣམ་པར་དག་པ་དང༌། སྡིག་དང་མ་འདྲེས་པ་སོགས་ཀྱི་སྦྱོར་བ་རྣམ་དག་གིས་བསྒྲུབས་པའི་རྣམ་པར་དཀར་བའི་ལས་དྲི་མེད་གངས་རི་ལྟ་བུ་ལས་སྐྱེས་པའི། ཡུལ་དང་དངོས་པོ་བྱེད་པ་སྟེ་འཁོར་གསུམ་གྱི་དམིགས་པའི་རྟུལ་གྱིས་རྙོག་པ་མེད་པའི་དགེ་ཚོགས་ཀྱི་ཆུ་རྒྱུན་རྣམས་གང་དུ་གཞོལ་ཞིང་འབབ་པའི་ཡུལ་ཆོས་སྐུ་ལོངས་སྐུ་སྤྲུལ་སྐུ་བདེ་བ་ཆེན་པོ་ངོ་བོ་ཉིད་སྐུ་སྟེ། རྒྱལ་བ་རྣམས་ཀྱི་སྐུ་བཞིའི་ངོ་བོ་ནི་ཟབ་ཅིང་རྒྱ་ཆེ་བས་རྒྱ་མཚོ་ལྟ་བུ་དེར་འཇུག་པར་གྱུར་ཅིག ཅེས་བསྔོ་དགོས་པར་འདོམ་པའི་ཕྱིར་སྨོན་པར་མཛད་པ་སྟེ་ཕྱི་མ་རྣམས་ལའང་ཤེས་པར་བྱའོ། །འཁོར་གསུམ་དམིགས་བྲལ་གྱི་ཤེས་རབ་དངོས་ནི་འཕགས་པའི་སྤྱོད་ཡུལ་ཡིན་ཀྱང་ལུང་དང་བླ་མའི་གདམས་ངག་གིས་རྗེས་མཐུན་རྟོགས་པ་ནི་སོ་སྐྱེ་ལའང་ཡོད་པར་གསུངས།

གཉིས་པ་བྱེ་བྲག་ཕྱེ་སྟེ་སྨོན་པ་ལ་ལྔ། ལམ་གྱི་རྟེན་ཕུན་ཚོགས་ལ་སྨོན་པ། ལམ་རྟོགས་བྱེད་ཀྱི་ཤེས་རབ་ལ་སྨོན་པ། འཁྲུལ་མེད་ཀྱི་ལམ་ལ་སྨོན་པ། ལམ་དེའི་ཉམས་ལེན་མ་འཁྲུལ་བ་ལ་སྨོན་པ། ལམ་མཐར་ཕྱིན་པའི་འབྲས་བུ་ལ་སྨོན་པའོ། །དང་པོ་ལ་ཐུན་མོང་དང༌། ཐུན་མིན་གཉིས་ལས། དང་པོ་ཐུན་མོང་ལམ་གྱི་རྟེན་ཕུན་ཚོགས་ལ་སྨོན་པ་ནི།

My totally pure thoughts and those of infinite sentient beings that are motivated by love, affection, faith, devotion, and so on, that are not mixed with a **mind** afflicted by three poisons, and the accomplishment of **totally pure deeds** not mixed with negativity and such, are totally white, immaculate karma like **the snow mountain**. Regarding place and things, **a stream** is the collected **virtues** that are **not muddied by** the sediment of reference to **the three spheres** of recipient, thing, and act. The place into which they fall is the dharmakāya, saṃbhogakāya, nirmāṇakāya, and mahāsukha svabhāvakāya. Since the essence of those **four kāyas** of all the **victors** is profound and vast, it is like **the ocean**. "**May it flow into** there" is the aspiration in order to encourage the necessary dedication. Know that this applies to all the future aspirations. Although the actual wisdom free of reference to the three spheres is the realm of activity of the noble ones, it is taught that a comparable realization based on the scriptures and guru's instructions are achieved by ordinary individuals.

B. The distinguishing particular explanations
These are divided into five: (1) aspiration for excellent support for the path, (2) aspiration for the wisdom that produces realization on the path, (3) aspiration for an undeluded true path, (4) aspiration for unmistaken practice on that path, and (5) aspiration for the ultimate result of the path.

(1) Aspiration for excellent support for the path
This has two parts: common and uncommon.

ཇི་སྲིད་དེ་མ་ཐོབ་པ་དེ་སྲིད་དུ། །ཁྱི་དང་སྐྱེ་བ་ཚེ་རབས་ཀུན་ཏུ། །
ཡང་། །ཕྱིག་དང་སྲུག་བསྐལ་སྐྱ་ཡང་མི་གྱག་ཅིང་། །བདེ་དགེ་རྒྱུ་
མཚོའི་དཔལ་ལ་སྤྱོད་པར་ཤོག །

།ཅེས་གསུངས་ཏེ། འདི་ནས་བཟུང་སྟེ་ཇི་ཙམ་སྲིད་པར་སྐྱེ་ཞིང་རྒྱལ་
བ་སྐུ་བཞིའི་གོ་འཕང་དམ་པ་དེ་མ་ཐོབ་པ་དེ་སྲིད་ཀྱི་བར་དུ་སྐྱེ་
དང་སྐྱེ་བའི་ཚེ་རབས་ཀུན་ཏུ་ཡང་རྒྱུ་ཕྱིག་པ་དང་འབྲས་བུ་སྲུག་
བསྐལ་གྱི་སྐུ་ཙམ་ཡང་མི་གྱག་ཅིང་བདེ་ཞིང་སྐྱིད་པ་དང་དེའི་རྒྱུ་
དགེ་བ་རྒྱ་མཚོ་ལྟ་བུའི་དཔལ་འབྱོར་ལ་ལོངས་སྤྱོད་པ་ཁོ་ན་ཤོག་
ཅིག་ཅེས་པའོ། །

།གཉིས་པ་ ཐུན་མིན་ལམ་གྱི་ཇེན་ཐུན་ཚོགས་ལ་སྟོན་པ་ནི།

དལ་འབྱོར་མཆོག་ཐོབ་དད་བརྩོན་ཤེས་རབ་ལྡན། །བཤེས་གཉེན་
བཟང་བསྟེན་གདམས་པའི་བཅུད་ཐོབ་ནས། །ཚུལ་བཞིན་བསྒྲུབ་ལ་
བར་ཆད་མ་མཆིས་པར། །ཚེ་རབས་ཀུན་ཏུ་དས་ཚོས་སྤྱོད་པར་ཤོག

།ཅེས་གསུངས་ཏེ། དེར་མ་ཟད་ཁྱད་པར་དུ་ཡང་བྱང་རྒྱབ་བསྒྲུབ་
ཅུང་གི་ཇེན་དལ་བརྒྱད་འབྱོར་བཅུ་ཚང་བའི་ཁམས་དྲུག་ལྡན་གྱི་
མིའི་ལུས་མཆོག་ཁོ་ན་ཐོབ་ཅིང་། ཇེན་འབྱུང་གི་ཚོས་ལས་འབྲས་ལ་
ཡིད་ཆེས་པའི་དད་པ། སངས་རྒྱས་ཀྱི་བྱང་རྒྱབ་ལ་འདོད་པའི་དད་
པ། བླ་མ་དགོན་མཆོག་ལ་དང་བའི་དད་པ་དང་། དགེ་བ་ལ་ཆེས་
སྨྲ་བའི་རྟག་སྤྱོར་དང་། གུས་སྤྱོར་གྱི་བཙོན་འགྲུས་དང་། འཇིག་ཇེན་
དང་འཇིག་ཇེན་ལས་འདས་པའི་ཤེས་བྱའི་ཚོས་ཐམས་ཅད་རབ་

a. Common aspiration

3. Until that comes to pass, however long it takes,
throughout life after life in the future,
with even the sounds "sin" and "suffering" unknown;
may I enjoy the glorious sea of happiness and virtue.

From now on **until however long it takes** to attain that sublime state of the victors' four kāyas, **throughout life after life in the the future**, we pray that **even the sounds** of the causal **sins** and the resultant **sufferings** be **unknown**, while **enjoying** only prosperity and **glorious happiness** and joy and their cause, which is like a **sea of virtue**.

b. Uncommon aspiration

4. Free and endowed; having faith, vigor, and wisdom,
attending a good spiritual master, receiving the nectar of
    teachings,
and properly practicing them without obstacles;
may I engage in the holy Dharma in all future lifetimes.

Not only that, you especially aspire to obtain only the support conducive to accomplishing awakening, which is the excellent human body with six constituents, and including all eight **freedoms and** ten **endowments**. You aspire to have [three kinds of faith:] the **faith** of belief in the functioning of cause and effect in interdependently arising phenomena, the faith of yearning for a buddha's awakening, and the faith of inspiration in the guru and Three Jewels. You aspire to have the **vigor** of constant application and devoted application to

ཏུ་འབྱེད་ནུས་ཀྱི་ཤེས་རབ་རྣམས་དང་ལྡན་པ་དང་། བླ་མེད་རྫོགས་
བྱང་དུ་འབྱེད་པའི་ལམ་མཁན་བླ་མ་དགེ་བའི་བཤེས་གཉེན་
མཚན་ཉིད་དང་ལྡན་པའི་བཟང་པོ་དང་ཕྲད་ནས་དེ་ཉིད་མཉེས་
པའི་ཞབས་ཏོག་དགུ་ཕྱགས་སོགས་མདོར་ན་བླ་མ་ལྷ་བཅུ་པ་ལས་
གསུངས་པ་ལྟར་ཚུལ་བཞིན་ཏུ་བསྟེན་པས། དེ་ཉིད་ལས་གདུལ་
བྱའི་ཁམས་དབང་དང་འཆམས་པའི་གདམ་ངག་ཐར་ལམ་གྱི་སྒྲོག་
འཇིན་པའི་བཅུད་ལྔན་པ་ཐོབ་ནས་ཐོབ་ལོ་ཚམ་དུ་མི་འཇོག་པར་
ཇི་སྐད་གདམས་པའི་ཆུལ་དེ་ཁོ་ན་བཞིན་དུ་བསྐྱལ་ཅིང་ཉམས་
སུ་ལེན་པ་དང་། དེ་ལ་ཕྱི་འགྱུབ་བ་བཞི་དང་མི་མ་ཡིན་སོགས་ཀྱི་
བར་ཆད་དང་། ནང་ནད་དང་ཉོན་མོངས་རྣམ་པར་རྟོག་པ་སོགས་
མདོར་ན་བྱང་ཆུབ་ཀྱི་ལམ་ལ་བར་ཆད་མཐའ་དག་མ་མཆིས་པར་
ཚེ་རབས་ཀྱི་ཕྲེང་བ་ཀུན་ཏུ་དགེ་ཆོས་རྣལ་མ་ལ་སྒྱོད་པའི་སྐལ་བ་
ཅན་ཁོ་ནར་འགྱུར་བར་ཤོག་ཅིག་ཅེས་པའོ། །

གཉིས་པ་ལམ་རྟོགས་བྱེད་ཀྱི་ཤེས་རབ་ལ་སྟོན་པ་ནི།

ཡུང་རིགས་ཐོས་པས་མི་ཤེས་སྒྲུབ་ལས་གྲོལ། །མན་ངག་བསམ་པས་
ཐེ་ཚོམ་མྱུན་ནག་བཅོམ། །བསྒོམས་བྱུང་འོད་ཀྱིས་གནས་ལུགས་ཇི་
བཞིན་གསལ། །ཤེས་རབ་གསུམ་གྱི་སྣང་བ་རྒྱས་པར་ཤོག །

eagerly pursue virtue. You aspire to have **wisdom** that can fully distinguish all mundane and transcendent knowable phenomena. Endowed with all those, you aspire to meet the guide who leads you to unsurpassed complete awakening, a holy guru with all the characteristics of **a good spiritual master**, and then offer all kinds of pleasing service and so on. This is, briefly, to **attend** that master properly according to the instructions in *Fifty Verses of Guru Devotion*.[20] From that person, the disciple **receives the** vitalizing **nectar** of the path to freedom as a **teaching** that is compatible with your constitution and capabilities. Once you obtain it, do not become complacent in thinking "I've got it." **Put it into practice properly** and accomplish it only in the way in which it was taught, **without** any external **obstacles** from the four elements or nonhumans and so forth, and without inner **obstacles** such as sickness, afflictions, and discursive thoughts. In short, we aspire only to become a fortunate one who **engages** in the genuine **holy Dharma** throughout the succession of **all future lifetimes**, free of all obstacles to the path of awakening.

(2) Aspiration for the wisdom that produces realization on the path

5. *Studying scripture and logic liberates from obscurations of*
    unknowing.
Contemplating esoteric instruction vanquishes doubt's
    darkness.
Light from meditation illuminates the abiding nature as it is.
May the brilliance of these three wisdoms increase.

ཅེས་གསུངས་ཏེ། རྟོགས་པའི་སངས་རྒྱས་ཀྱི་ཞལ་ནས་གསུངས་པ་
རྗེས་སུ་གནང་བ་བྱིན་གྱིས་རླབས་པའི་བཀའ་གསུམ་མམ། བརྗོད་
བྱའི་དབང་དུ་ན་སྟེ་སྟོང་གསུམ་སྟེ་བཀའ་དང༌། དེའི་དགོངས་འགྲེལ་
སྟེ་དང་བྲི་བྲག་སོགས་བསྟན་བཅོས་ཀྱི་ལུང་དང༌། ཆད་མའི་དམ་
བཅའ་དང་གཏན་ཚིགས་དང་དཔེ་སོགས་ཀྱི་སྒྲོ་ནས་གཏན་ལ་ཕབ་
པས་རྟོགས་བྱ་གང་ཡིན་གྱི་དོན་སྟིའི་ཆུལ་གྱིས་ཤེས་བྱེད་རིགས་པ་
བཅས་སྣ་མ་ལས་ཐོས་པར་བྱས་པས་ཐོས་བྱུང་གི་ཤེས་རབ་སྐྱེས་
ཏེ། དེའི་མི་མཐུན་ཕྱོགས་ལུང་རིགས་མི་ཤེས་པའི་སྒྲིབ་པ་ལས་གྲོལ་
བ་དང༌། མདོ་རྒྱུད་དགོངས་འགྲེལ་དང་བཅས་པའི་དོན་དྲང་ངེས་
དགོངས་ཕྱེམ་དགོངས་དང་ཁྱད་པར་བླ་མེད་ཀྱི་རྒྱུད་མཐའ་དྲུག
ཚུལ་བཞིས་བཅིངས་པ་རྣམས་མཚོན་ལྔན་བླ་མས་ཆུལ་བཞིན་ཕྱེས་
ཏེ་གདམས་པའི་མན་ངག་རྣམས་རང་རྒྱུད་དང་སྦྱར་ཏེ་ཆུལ་བཞིན་
བསམ་པས་བསམ་བྱུང་གི་ཤེས་རབ་སྐྱེས་ཏེ་དེའི་ལྟོག་ཕྱོགས་ཟབ་
མོའི་གནས་ལ་སེམས་རྩེ་གཉིས་པའི་ཐེ་ཚོམ་གྱི་མུན་ནག་བཙོམ་པ་
དང༌། མང་དུ་ཐོས་ཤིང་དོན་ཆུལ་བཞིན་བསམ་པས་ངེས་པ་རྙེད་
པ་དེ་ཉིད་ལ་རྩེ་གཅིག་ཏུ་མཉམ་པར་བཞག་ཅིང་གོམས་པར་བྱས་
པས་སྒོམ་བྱུང་གི་ཤེས་རབ་སྐྱེས་ཏེ་དེའི་འོད་ཀྱིས་གཟུགས་ནས་རྣམ་
མཁྱེན་བར་གྱི་ཆོས་ཐམས་ཅད་ཀྱི་རང་བཞིན་ནམ་གནས་ལུགས་དེ་
ཉིད་ཇི་ལྟ་བ་བཞིན་དུ་གསལ་བ་དང༌། དེ་ལྟར་ཐོས་བསམ་སྒོམ་བྱུང་
གི་ཤེས་རབ་གསུམ་གྱི་རང་འོད་སྣང་བ་ཆེན་པོ་ཉིད་དུ་རྒྱས་པས་དེ་
ཁོ་ན་ཉིད་ཀྱི་རང་བཞིན་མཛོན་སུམ་དུ་མཐོང་བར་ཕོག་ཅིག་ཅེས་
པའོ།

There are three kinds of Buddha Word: the words spoken directly by the perfect Buddha, those of which he approved, and those with his blessing. Or, in terms of subject matter, there are the three baskets (*Tripiṭaka*) of precepts, as well as the treatises that comment in general and in particular on their intent. This is **scripture**. **Logic** is to ascertain the truth by means of the logical theses of valid cognition, syllogisms, metaphors, and so on, that enable you to understand in a general fashion the meaning of whatever is to be realized. The wisdom that comes from **studying** with the guru arises and you are **liberated** from its opposite, the **obscuration** of **not knowing** scripture and logic.

An authentic guru distinguishes the meaning of sutras, tantras, and their commentaries as definitive, provisional, intentional, or having concealed intentions. Especially with regard to the highest yoga tantra, [the guru applies] the clinchers of the six limits and four modes.[21] The [disciple] applies those teachings of **esoteric instructions** to their own mindstream and properly **contemplates** them, giving rise to the wisdom that comes from contemplation, and **vanquishes** its opposite, the **darkness of** conflicted **doubt** concerning profound topics.

You will find certitude through much studying and proper contemplation of the meaning. The wisdom that comes **from meditation** will arise through resting in single-focused equipoise on just that and becoming accustomed to it. Its **light** will **illuminate** the intrinsic nature of all phenomena, from form up through omniscience, or **the abiding nature** of suchness **just as it is**. Thus, we aspire to see the intrinsic nature of suchness through the vast **increase** of great brilliance of the innate light of the **three wisdoms** that come from study, contemplation, and meditation.

།དེའང་གཞི་དུས་ཀྱི་ཕྱག་ཆེན་གཏུག་མའི་དེ་ཉིད་དང་པོའི་མགོན་
པོ། སེམས་ཀྱི་རྡོ་རྗེ། བདེ་གཤེགས་སྙིང་པོ་སོགས་རྣམ་གྲངས་དུ་མས་
བསྟན་པ་དེ་ཉིད་ལའང་ལུས་དངོས་པོའི་གནས་ལུགས་དང་སེམས་
དངོས་པོའི་གནས་ལུགས་གཉིས་ལས། སྣ་མ་ནི་ཀུན་རྫོབ་བྱུང་སེམས་
ལས་གྲུབ་པ་སྐྱང་བ་མཆོག་ཏུ་མི་འགྱུར་བའི་བདེ་བའི་རྟེན་རྩ་རླུང་
ཐིག་ལེའི་དྭངས་མ་ཧཱ་ཧྲྀལ་གྱི་ཚོས་ལས་འདས་པས་ཡེ་ཤེས་ཀྱི་རྡོ་རྡོར་
གྱུར་པ་གཏུག་མའི་ལུས་དང་རྒྱུས་འགྱུར་གྱི་རིགས་ཞེས་ཚོས་རྗེ་གཙུག་
པ་ཡབ་སྲས་བཞེད་ཅིང་། ཕྱི་མ་ནི་རྒྱུ་ཆད་ཕྱོགས་ལྷུང་གི་སྟོས་མཐའ་
བྲལ་བའི་ཚོས་དབྱིངས་ཟབ་གསལ་གཉིས་མེད་གཏུག་མའི་སེམས་
དང་རང་བཞིན་གནས་རིགས་ཞེས་པ་ཉིད་དེ་ལུས་སེམས་ཀྱི་གཞིའི་
གནས་ལུགས་དེ་གཉིས་རྒྱུ་དང་འགྱུག་སྐྱམ་བཞིན་དབྱེར་མི་ཕྱེད་
པས་གཞི་དུས་ཀྱི་སྐུ་གཉིས་ཟུང་འཇུག་ཅེས་བྱ་ཞིང་། དེ་ཉིད་བྱིན་
རླབས་དང་སྟོབ་སྟོབས་ཀྱི་རང་རིག་མངོན་སུམ་ཁོ་ནས་གསལ་བར་
ཉམས་ཀྱི་ཐབས་གཞན་གྱིས་མ་ཡིན་པར་གསུངས་སོ། །

གསུམ་པ་འབྲལ་མེད་ཀྱི་ལམ་ཉིད་ལ་སློན་པ་ནི།

རྟག་ཆད་མཐའ་བྲལ་བདེན་གཉིས་གཞི་ཡི་དོན། །སྒོ་སྐུར་མཐའ་
བྲལ་ཚོགས་གཉིས་ལམ་མཆོག་གིས། །སྲིད་ཞིའི་མཐའ་བྲལ་དོན་
གཉིས་འབྲས་ཐོབ་པའི། །གོལ་འཆུག་མེད་པའི་ཚོས་དང་འཕྲད་པར་
ཤོག

There are many synonyms that have been used, such as ground-state mahāmudrā, innate suchness, original lord, mind vajra, buddha nature, and so forth. Also there is the abiding nature of the body entity and the abiding nature of the mind entity. The former refers to the support of penultimate bliss that appears through relative bodhicitta—the refined essence of the channels, vital winds, and vital drops that transcend material phenomena and so are essentially timeless awareness. That is called the "innate body" (*gnyug ma'i lus*) and "developed affinity" (*rgyas 'gyur gyi rigs*), as explained by the lord Karmapa, father and sons. The latter is the realm of phenomena free of the limits of elaborations, partiality, and prejudice; the nondual profundity and clarity, also called "innate mind" and "the intrinsically abiding affinity." Those two abiding natures of the ground of body and mind are indivisible, like water and ice. So they are called "the unity of the two kāyas at the ground state." It is said that this itself can only be illuminated through reflexive awareness manifested by blessings and the power of meditation, and not by any other means.

(3) Aspiration for an undeluded path

6. *"Ground" means the two truths free of extreme eternalism or*
    nihilism.
"Supreme path" is two accumulations free of extreme imposi-
    tion or denial.
This leads to the result: the two benefits free of extreme existence
    or peace.
May I meet the Dharma without deviation or error.

།ཅེས་གསུངས་ཏེ། དོན་དམ་བདེན་པ་བརྟན་གཡོ་འབྱོར་འདས་ཀྱི་
ཆོས་གང་སྐྱང་ཐམས་ཅད་སྐྱང་དུས་ཉིད་ནས་དེའི་ངོ་བོར་ཡོད་
མ་མྱོང་བ་མེ་ལོང་གི་གཟུགས་བརྙན་ལྟ་བུར་རྟག་པའི་མཐའ་དང་
བྲལ་ཞིང་། ཀུན་རྫོབ་བདེན་པ་ངོ་བོ་སྟོང་ཉིད་ལས་མ་གཡོས་བཞིན་
དུ་སྐྱང་བ་སྣ་ཚོགས་འགག་མེད་དུ་འཆར་བས་ཆད་པའི་མཐའ་
དང་བྲལ་བའི་བདེན་གཉིས་གདོད་ནས་བྱུང་དུ་འཇུག་པའི་ཤེས་
བྱ་གཞིའི་གནས་ལུགས་ཀྱི་དོན་འབྱལ་མེད་དུ་རྟོགས་པ་དང་། སྐྱང་
བའི་ཆོས་ཁོ་ནར་ཞེན་ནས་སྟོང་ཉིད་ལས་རྟེན་འབྲེལ་དུ་ཤར་ཚུལ་
མ་ཤེས་པར་ཤེས་རབ་ཀྱི་ཚ་སྟོང་བ་མེད་པ་ལ་ཡོད་པར་སྒྲོ་བཏགས་
པའི་མཐའ་དང་། སྟོང་ཉིད་ཁོ་ནར་ཞེན་ནས་དགོན་མཆོག་ལས་
འབྲས་སོགས་རྟེན་འབྱུང་གི་ཆོས་སྣང་ངོ་ཚམ་དུ་དོན་བྱེད་ནུས་ཀྱི་
གནད་མ་ཤེས་པར་ཐབས་ཀྱི་ཚ་སྟོང་བ་ཡོད་པ་ལ་མེད་པར་སྐུར་
འདེབས་ཀྱི་མཐའ་སྟེ་མཐའ་དེ་གཉིས་དང་བྲལ་བས་ཐབས་བསོད་
ནམས་ཀྱི་ཚོགས་དང་ཤེས་རབ་ཡེ་ཤེས་ཀྱི་ཚོགས་ཏེ་ཚོགས་གཉིས་
ཕྱོགས་རིས་མིན་པར་བྱུང་འཇུག་དུ་བསྐྱབ་པ་ལྷ་མེད་བྱུང་ཆུབ་
འཐོབ་པའི་ལམ་མཆོག་ཏུ་གྱུར་པ་དག་གིས། སྲིད་པའི་མཐར་མ་
ལྷུང་བ་རང་དོན་ཕུན་ཚོགས་གཟུགས་ཀྱི་སྐུ་དང་། ཞི་བའི་མཐར་མ་
ལྷུང་བ་གཞན་དོན་ཕུན་ཚོགས་གཟུགས་ཀྱི་སྐུ་སྟེ་འབྲས་བུ་སྐུ་གཉིས་
བྱུང་འཇུག་ཐོབ་པའི་གནད་གཞི་ལམ་འབྲས་གསུམ་གྱི་མཐའ་གཉིས་
དང་བྲལ་ཏེ་གོལ་འཆུག་མེད་པའི་ཆོས་ཡང་དག་པ་དང་དེ་སྟོན་
པའི་བླ་མ་དམ་པ་དང་འཕྲད་པར་ཤོག་ཅིག་ཅེས་པའོ། །

The ultimate truth is that one cannot experience the existence of an essence in any appearing phenomena of samsara and nirvana, animate or inanimate, from the very moment that they appear, as with the reflections in a mirror. This is **freedom from the extreme of eternalism**. The relative truth is that various appearances arise unhindered without actually shifting away from their empty essence. This is freedom from the **extreme of nihilism**. The knowledge that these two truths are united from the beginning is the undeluded realization of the **meaning of the ground**'s abiding nature.

Cleaving only to apparent phenomena while neglecting the wisdom aspect without understanding the way that interdependence arises from emptiness is the **extreme** of **superimposition** that imposes existence on nonexistence. Cleaving only to emptiness while neglecting the method aspect, and thinking that the Three Jewels and karmic cause and effect and such are merely the apparent phenomena of interdependence without understanding the vital point of their functionality, is the **extreme** of **denial** that denies the existence of what exists. **Free of** those **two extremes**, the practice of the **two accumulations**—the accumulation of merit and the accumulation of wisdom-awareness—as a unity without bias is the **supreme path** for attaining unsurpassed awakening.

Those who [follow that path] do not fall into the **extreme of** [conditioned] **existence** and attain the dharmakāya of abundant **benefit** for themselves, and do not fall into the **extreme of peace** and attain the rūpakāya of abundant benefit for others. The vital point is the attainment of **the result**: two kāyas united. Free of the dualistic extremes of all the three—ground, path, and result—we aspire to **meet** the genuine **Dharma without deviation or error** and the holy guru who teaches it.

བཞི་པ་ལམ་དེའི་ཉམས་སུ་ལེན་ཚུལ་ལ་འཁྲུལ་བར་སྟོན་པ་ལ།
གཉིས། གོ་དོན་དང་། སྐྱོན་དོན་ནོ། །དང་པོ་ཤོ་དོན་ར་ནི།

སྒྲུང་གཞི་སེམས་ཉིད་གསལ་སྟོང་རྲུང་འཇུག་ལ། །སྟོང་བྱེད་ཕྱག་
ཆེན་རྫོ་རྗེའི་རྣལ་འབྱོར་ཆེས། །སྒྲུང་བུ་བློ་བུར་འཁྲུལ་པའི་དྲི་མ་
རྣམས། །སྒྱངས་འབྲས་དྲི་བྲལ་ཆོས་སྐུ་མངོན་འགྱུར་ཤོག

།ཅེས་གསུངས་ཏེ། འཕོར་བར་འཁྲུལ་པའི་དྲི་མ་སྒྲུང་བའི་གཞི་ནི།
སྣོབ་དཔོན་ཀླུ་ཞབས་ཀྱིས། ས་བོན་གྱུར་པའི་ཁམས་དེ་ཉིད། །ཆོས་
རྣམས་ཀུན་གྱི་རྟེན་དུ་འདོད། །རིམ་གྱིས་སྒྲངས་པར་གྱུར་པ་ལས། །
།མངས་རྒྱས་གོ་འཕང་འཐོབ་པར་གྱུར། །ཞེས་སོགས་ལུང་མཐའ་
ཡས་པའི་ཁམས་སམ་གཤེགས་སྙིང་ངམ་སེམས་ཉིད་ཀྱི་རྫོ་རྗེ་ཞེས་
པ་རང་བཞིན་འགགག་མེད་དུ་གསལ་ཡང་ཏོ་པོ་གཞི་མེད་རྩ་བྲལ་
དུ་སྟོང་པའི་གསལ་སྟོང་རྲུང་འཇུག་གི་མཚན་ཉིད་ཅན་དེ་ཡིན་
ལ། དེའི་སྟེང་གི་དྲི་མ་སྟོང་བྱེད་ཀྱི་ཐབས་ནི་འདིར་ཧིང་ཏུ་ཆེན་པོ་
མཉམ་མེད་དུ་གས་པོ་བཀའ་བརྒྱུད་ཀྱི་གདམས་སྲོལ་ཕྱག་ཆེན་རྫོ་
རྗེའི་རྣལ་འབྱོར་ཆེན་པོས་བདེ་བྲག་ཏུ་སྟོང་སྟེ། སྒྲུང་བར་བུ་རྒྱུའི་དྲི་
མའང་སྒྲུང་གཞིའི་གཉིས་ལ་མེད་ཀྱང་བློ་བུར་འཁྲུལ་པས་བསྐྱེད་
པའི་དྲི་མ་གཟུང་འཛིན་གྱི་ཆོས་རྣམས་ཡིན་ཅིང་། དེ་སྒྲངས་པའི་
འབྲས་བུ་གཉིས་སྣང་གཟུང་འཛིན་གྱི་དྲི་མ་མཐའ་དག་དང་བྲལ་

(4) Aspiration for unmistaken practice on that path
This has two parts: theory and practice.

a. The theory to understand

7. The ground of refining is mind itself, the unity of
   clarity-emptiness.

The refiner is the great vajra yoga of mahāmudrā.
It refines the object, the stains of incidental delusion.
May I actualize the refined result, stainless dharmakāya.

The ground upon which the stains of samsaric delusion are
refined was taught by Master Nāgārjuna:

> That very seed that becomes the constituent
> is asserted to be the basis of all qualities.
> Buddhahood will be attained
> through its gradual refinement.[22]

This and endless scriptures speak of the constituent or the
buddha nature or the vajra of mind itself. These refer to that
which is characterized by **the unity of clarity** and **emptiness**—clarity that is unimpeded intrinsic nature while empty
of a basis or root essence. The method for **refining** the stains
that accrue to it is presented here from **the great vajra yoga of
mahāmudrā** in the convenient instruction system of the great
chariot of the unequaled Dakpo Kagyü. The stains that are
to be **refined** don't actually exist in the fundamental disposition (*gshis*) of the ground of refinement. However, **stains** arise
from **incidental delusions**, producing all phenomena of dualistic subject–object clinging. We aspire to attain the **result of**

བའི་གཉིས་མེད་ཡེ་ཤེས་ཀྱི་ཚོས་སྐུ་མངོན་སུམ་དུ་འགྱུར་བར་ཐོག་
ཅིག་ཅེས་པའོ། །ཚོས་སྐུ་དེ་འང་རང་བཞིན་རྣམ་དག་ལ་སྒྲོ་བུར་གྱི་
དྲི་མ་འང་དག་པས་དག་པ་གཉིས་ལྡན་ནི་སྱངས་པ་ཚོས་སྐུའམ་དོ་
བོ་ཉིད་སྐུ་དང་ཀུན་གཞི། ཏོན་ཡིད། དྲུག་ཡིད། སྒོ་ལྔའི་རྣམ་ཤེས་
རྣམས་ཡོངས་སུ་དག་ཅིང་གནས་གྱུར་པ་ནི་མཁྱེན་པ་གཉིས་ལྡན་
གྱི་ཡེ་ཤེས་རྟོགས་པ་ཚོས་སྐུའམ་ཡེ་ཤེས་ཀྱི་སྐུ་སྟེ་སྱངས་རྟོགས་ཀྱི་
སྐུ་གཉིས་དབྱེར་མེད་པ་ནི་ཚོས་སྐུ་ཡོངས་སུ་རྟོགས་པ་ཡིན་ལ་ཕྱི་
མ་ལ་དག་བྱ་རྣམ་ཤེས་དེ་རྣམས་ཀྱི་རིས་པས་མེ་ལོང༌། མཉམ་ཉིད།
སོར་རྟོག་བྱ་གྲུབ་སྟེ་ཡེ་ཤེས་བཞི་དང་སྐུ་གསུམ་དུ་དབྱེ་བའོ། །

གཉིས་པ་སྐོམ་དོན་ལག་ཏུ་ལེན་པའི་སྐོན་ལམ་ལ། བཤད་
གཉིས་ལས། དང་པོ་མངོར་བསྟན་པ་ནི།

གཞི་ལ་སྒྲོ་འདོགས་ཚོད་པ་ལྟ་བའི་གདེང་། །དེ་ལ་མ་ཡེངས་སྐྱོང་བ་
སྒོམ་པའི་གནད། །སྒོམ་དོན་ཀུན་ལ་རྩལ་སྦྱོང་སྤྱོད་པའི་མཆོག །ལྟ་
སྒོམ་སྤྱོད་པའི་གདིང་དང་ལྡན་པར་ཤོག །ཅེས་གསུངས་ཏེ།

refinement, the **actualization** of the **dharmakāya** of nondual timeless awareness, **free of all stains** of dualistic appearance.

The purification (*dag pa*) of incidental stains that accrue to the totally pure intrinsic nature of the dharmakāya leads to having twofold purity (*dag pa gnyis ldan*). That is the abandonment dharmakāya or the svabhāvakāya. The fundamental transformation (*gnas gyur*) from the complete purification of the all-base, afflicted mentality, sixth mental consciousness, and the consciousnesses of the five organs leads to the realized timeless awareness with twofold knowledge (*mkhyen pa gnyis ldan*), which is the dharmakāya or jñānakāya. The inseparability of the two kāyas of abandonment and realization is the completely perfect dharmakāya. Regarding the latter, the consciousnesses that are to be purified are, in order, categorized into the four timeless awarenesses—mirror, equality, discerning, and accomplished—and the three kāyas.

b. The meditation to practice
The aspiration of taking up the practice of meditation has two parts: the presentation and the explanation.

i. Brief presentation

8. *Deep confidence in the view is to sever impositions on the
    ground.*
*The vital point of meditation is to hold that without
    distraction.*
Best conduct is to exercise skill in all meanings of meditation.
May I have deep confidence in view, meditation, and conduct.

ཕྱག་རྒྱ་ཆེན་པོ་ཉམས་སུ་ལེན་པ་ལ་དང་པོར་གཞི་གནས་ལུགས་
ཕྱག་ཆེན་ལ་སྒྲོ་འདོགས་ཆོད་དེ་ངེས་པ་རྙེད་པ་ལྟ་བའི་གཏིང་དང་
ལུན་ཞིང་ལྟ་བ་དེ་ཉིད་ལ་མཉམ་པར་བཞག་སྟེ་མ་ཡེངས་པར་སྐྱོང་
བ་སྒོམ་པའི་གནད་ལ་མཁས་ཤིང་ཇེ་སྐྱད་གསུངས་པའི་སྒོམ་དོན་
ཀུན་ལ་གོམས་ཤིང་འདྲིས་པར་རྩལ་སྦྱོང་པས་ནི་པོགས་མྱུར་དུ་ཐོན་
པར་འགྱུར་བས་སྦྱོད་པའི་མཚོག་ཏུ་གྱུར་པ་སྟེ། ལྟ་སྒོམ་སྦྱོད་པའི་
གནད་དེ་དག་ཆིག་ཆམ་དུ་མ་ལུས་པར་རང་རྒྱུད་ལ་མཛོན་དུ་གྱུར་
པའི་གཏིང་དང་ལྟན་པར་ཐོག་ཅིག་ཅེས་པའོ། །

གཉིས་པ་རྒྱས་པར་བྱེ་སྟེ་སྟོན་པ་ལ་གསུམ། ལྟ་བའི་སྒོ་འདོགས་
བཅད། སྒོམ་པས་ཉམས་སུ་བླངས། སྦྱོད་པས་མཐར་དབྱུང་བའོ།
།དང་པོ་ལའང་མདོར་བསྟན་པ་དང་། རྒྱས་པར་བྱེ་བ་གཉིས་ལས།
དང་པོ་ [མདོར་བསྟན་པ་] ནི།

ཆོས་རྣམས་ཐམས་ཅད་སེམས་ཀྱི་རྩལ་འཕྱལ་ཏེ། །སེམས་ནི་སེམས་
མེད་སེམས་ཀྱི་ངོ་བོས་སྟོང་། །སྟོང་ཞིང་མ་འགགས་ཅིར་ཡང་སྣང་བ་
སྟེ། །ལེགས་པར་བརྟགས་ནས་གཞི་རྩ་ཆོད་པར་ཤོག །

ཅེས་གསུངས་ཏེ། ཆིག་ཀུང་དང་པོས་སྣང་བ་ཐམས་ཅད་སེམས་
ཀྱི་རྩལ་འཕྱལ་དུ་ཐག་བཅད། གཉིས་པས་སེམས་རང་བཞིན་མེད་

In the practice of mahāmudrā, first you must **sever impositions on the ground** or abiding nature of mahāmudrā. In finding such certainty, you gain **deep confidence in the view**. Then to rest in equipoise in that view itself, **holding it without distraction**, you become skilled in the **vital point of meditation**. **Exercising skill** by getting acquainted and familiar with all the **meanings of meditation** just as they were taught quickly enhances [the experience], leading to the **best conduct**. We aspire to have the **deep confidence** of actualizing the vital points of **view, meditation, and conduct** in the mindstream and not just in words.

ii. Extensive analysis
This explains three parts in the aspiration here: severing superimpositions of the view, practicing through meditation, and consummating through conduct.

A) Severing superimpositions of the view
This has two parts: a brief presentation and an extensive explanation.

1) Brief presentation

9. *All phenomena are projections of the mind.*
As for mind, there is no mind—it is empty of an essence.
But, while empty, it appears freely as anything at all.
Examining this thoroughly, may I sever its base and roots.

The first line establishes that all appearing **phenomena** are the **projections of mind**. The second ascertains that the **mind** has **no** intrinsic nature. The third shows that **emptiness** and

པར་གཏན་ལ་ཕབ། གསུམ་པས་སྟོང་དང་ཉེན་འབྱུང་བྱུང་འཛུག་
མི་འགལ་བར་བསྟན། བཞི་པས་དེ་ལྟར་སོར་ཆོག་གི་ཉེས་རབ་ཀྱིས་
བཏགས་པས་གཞིའི་དོན་ལ་སྒྲོ་འདོགས་གཅོད་དགོས་པ་ལ་སྐྱོན་
པའོ། །

གཉིས་པ་དེ་རྒྱས་པར་བྱེ་བ་ལའང་དེ་ལྟར་བཞི་ལས། དང་པོ་སྐྱང་
བ་སེམས་སུ་ཐག་བཅད་པ་ནི།

ཡོད་མ་སྐྱོང་བའི་རང་སྐྱང་ཡུལ་དུ་འཁྲུལ། །མ་རིག་དབང་གིས་རང་
རིག་བདག་དུ་འཁྲུལ། །གཉིས་འཛིན་དབང་གིས་སྲིད་པའི་སྐྱོང་དུ་
འཁྱམས། །མ་རིག་འཁྲུལ་པའི་རྩད་དར་ཆོད་པར་ཤོག

།ཅེས་གསུངས་ཏེ། འོད་གསལ་སེམས་ཀྱི་རྫོ་རྗེ་པོ་སྟོང་ཞིང་རང་
བཞིན་གསལ་བས་རྣམ་པ་འགག་མེད་དུ་ཤར་བ་ཉིད་རང་དང་
དུས་སྙུ་ཕྱི་མེད་པར་ལྷན་ཅིག་སྐྱེས་པའི་མ་རིག་པ་གསེར་དང་
གཡའ་ལྷུ་བུའི་དྲི་མས་བསྒྲིབས་ཏེ། རང་གི་རྫོ་བོ་རང་རྒྱལ་གྱིས་
མ་རིག་པས་འདུ་བྱེད་ཀྱི་ཡིད་གཡོས། རྣམ་ཤེས་སྐྱེས་ཏེ་ཡུལ་དང་
འཛིན་པ་གཉིས་སུ་སྐྱང་བ་རང་གིས་རང་ལ་གཏད་ཅིང་བཟུང་སྟེ།
འཁྲུལ་བའི་བག་ཆགས་རེ་ཆེར་རྒྱས་ནས་ཉེན་འཕྲེལ་བཅུ་གཉིས་
ཀྱིས་བྱ་དང་སྒོ་ང་ལྟར་འཕོར་བ་སྟེ། དག་པའི་སེམས་ཉིད་ཀྱི་རང་
གཉིས་ལ་ཡེ་ནས་ཡོད་མ་སྐྱོང་བའི་རང་རྒྱལ་ལས་ནེ་བར་སྐྱང་བའི་
རང་བཞིན་གསལ་བའི་ཆ་ལ་དེ་ལྟར་དུ་མ་རྟོགས་པས་རང་གི་རང་
ལ་ཕྱི་དོན་ཡུལ་གཞན་དུ་བཟུང་སྟེ་འཁྲུལ་ཞིང་། མ་རིག་པའི་དབང་

interdependence are a unity and not a contradiction. The fourth makes the aspiration that it is necessary to **sever** superimpositions by **examining** with discriminating wisdom.

2) Extensive explanation
The first of four parts:

a) Establishing that all appearances are the projections of mind

10. *Mind's displays that never existed are mistaken for objects.*
Innate awareness is ignorantly mistaken for a self.
We wander in the expanse of existence by such dualism.
May I get to the bottom of delusional mistakes.

The vajra mind of lucid clarity is empty in essence, lucid by nature, and arises unimpededly in form. Innate ignorance arises simultaneously, neither before nor after. Like dross on gold, it is obscured by stains. Its dynamic energy is ignorant of its own essence, so a formative cognition stirs. Consciousness is born, and then the dualistic perception that fixates on object and subject. One regards oneself and grasps that [as an object]. The habitual pattern of delusion increases more and more and one circles around in the twelve links of interdependence like the chicken and the egg.

The innate dynamic energy (*rang rtsal*) of the innate disposition (*rang gshis*) of pure **mind** itself **that never existed displays** itself as subjective appearance (*nye bar snang ba*). Through not realizing that appearance as the clarity aspect of your intrinsic nature, you subjectively grasp yourself as an external **object**—an other—and are thus **mistaken**. Under

གིས་རང་རིག་གཞི་མེད་རྩ་བྲལ་དུ་མ་རྟོགས་པར་ཉོན་མོངས་པའི་

ཡིད་ཀྱིས་ཡུལ་འཛིན་པ་པོ་ངང་སྐྱམ་དུ་ང་པོ་སྟོང་པའི་ཆ་ལ་བདག་

དུ་རྟོག་སྟེ་འབྱུང་ནས། བདག་གཞན་གཉིས་སྣང་གཟུང་འཛིན་གྱི་

རྟོག་པས་ཆགས་སྡང་རྨོངས་གསུམ་སྐྱེས། དེས་ལས་བསགས་ཏེ་དེའི་

དབང་གིས་སྲིད་གསུམ་འཁོར་བའི་སྐྱོང་དུ་འཁྱམས་པ་ཡིན་པས་

ན་གཟུང་འཛིན་གཉིས་བསྱས་ཀྱི་ཚོས་ཐམས་ཅད་འཁྲུལ་བ་ཁོ་ན་

ཡིན་ལ་འཁྲུལ་གཞིའང་སེམས་ཡིན་པས། སེམས་ལས་ལོགས་སུ་ཧྲལ་

ཚམ་མ་གྲུབ་སྟེ། དཔེ་སྤྲགས་ཀྱི་སྟོང་བས་ནམ་མཁའ་ལ་རྟ་གླང་སྱང་

བ་ལྟ་བུའོ། །དེས་ན་མ་རིག་པའི་དབང་གིས་ཇི་ལྟར་འཁྲུལ་ཚུལ་

མ་ཤེས་ན་འཁྲུལ་བར་མི་མཐོང་ཞིང་། དེ་མ་མཐོང་ན་སྟོང་དུ་མི་

བཅུབ་པའི་ཕྱིར་དེའི་གནད་ཅུད་དང་ཚོད་པར་ཐོག་ཅིག་ཅེས་པའོ།

།དེ་ལྟར་ཐོག་མེད་ནས་ཡ་འཐས་ཀྱི་བག་ཆགས་གོམས་ཆེས་པས་

འཁོར་བའི་ཚོས་དངོས་སྣང་རགས་པ་འདི་རྣམས་སེམས་ཀྱི་གནས་

ཚུལ་དང་ཤིན་དུ་འགལ་བ་ལྟར་འདུག་པ་འདི་སེམས་སུ་གཏན་ལ་

ཕེབས་ན། ཕྲ་བ་རྣམ་བྱང་གི་ཚོས་རྣམས་ནི་སེམས་ཀྱི་གནས་ཚུལ་

དང་རྗེས་སུ་མཐུན་པས་བདེ་བླག་དུ་ཤེས་པའི་ཕྱིར་ཕྱགས་ལ་བསྩན་

པ་སྟེ། དེས་ན་རྣམ་བྱང་གི་ཚོས་ཐམས་ཅད་ཀྱང་དག་པའི་སེམས་

ཀྱི་རང་བཞིན་ལས་མ་འདས་ཏེ། དྲི་བཅུས་ཀྱི་སྐབས་སུ་སེམས་ཡིད་

རྣམ་ཤེས་གསུམ་པོ་དྲི་བྲལ་གྱི་ཆ་སྐྱུ་གསུམ་དུ་རྣམ་པར་འཛོགས་

པའི་ཕྱིར། ལམ་གྱི་སྐབས་སུ་སྒྲུབ་བྱེའི་དྲི་མ་རྗེ་སྲུབ་དུ་སོང་བཞིན་དག་

པའི་སེམས་ལ་གནས་པའི་ཡོན་ཏན་རྗེ་གསལ་དུ་འགྱུར་ཞིང་དྲི་

མ་ཐམས་ཅད་དག་ཆེ་གཞིའི་ཡོན་ཏན་ཐམས་ཅད་སྣང་བ་རྒྱུད་བླ

the influence of this **ignorance**, the afflicted mentation that does not realize that **innate awareness** (*rang rig*) is ground-less and rootless thinks that the one who subjectively grasps objects is "I" and conceives of the empty essence aspect as **a self**, again being **mistaken**. With such concepts of **dualistic** subject–object appearances of self and other, the three afflic-tions of attraction, aversion, and neutral stupidity are born. With that, you accumulate karma and under its power you become a **wanderer in the expanse** of the three cyclic **exis-tences**. Therefore, all phenomena included in subject–object dualism are only delusion. But the basis of delusion is mind. Apart from the mind, not a single atom is established as exis-tent. For instance, it is like the magical appearances of horses and elephants in the sky produced by applying mantra. There-fore if, under the power of **ignorance**, you do not understand the way you are **mistakenly deluded**, then you do not see it as delusion. Since you cannot eliminate what you cannot see, we aspire to **get to the bottom** of that vital point.

In that way, the powerful conditioning of habitual pat-terns of reification since beginningless time have caused these coarse manifest appearances of samsaric phenomena, which are like the total opposite of the mind's way of abiding. When these are ascertained as mind, the subtle totally pure phenom-ena which *are* consistent with the abiding nature of mind are easy to understand, so that is revealed implicitly. Therefore, all perfectly pure phenomena do not transcend the intrinsic nature of the pure mind. At the time of having stains, there is the triad of all-ground, afflicted mentation, and conscious-ness.[23] From the stainless aspect, these are classified as the three kāyas. Therefore, at the time of the path, as the stains that are to be refined grow weaker, the qualities that dwell

ཨ་ལས་གསུངས་པ་ལྟར་རོ། །རྒྱུ་མཚན་འདིས་གདུལ་བྱའི་ཤེས་རྒྱུད་
དག་རིམ་གྱིས་སངས་རྒྱས་སྐུ་གསུམ་མཐོང་བའང་ཤེས་པར་བྱའོ། །

གཉིས་པ་སེམས་རང་བཞིན་མེད་པར་གཏན་ལ་འབེབས་པ་ལ་
གཉིས། ཡོད་མེད་དང་ཡིན་མིན་གྱི་མཐའ་སྤོང་བའོ། །དང་པོ་ཡོད་
མེད་ཀྱི་མཐའ་སྤོང་བ་ད་ནི།

ཡོད་པ་མ་ཡིན་རྒྱལ་བས་ཀྱང་མ་གཟིགས། །མེད་པ་མ་ཡིན་འཁོར་
འདས་ཀུན་གྱི་གཞི། །འགལ་འདུ་མ་ཡིན་ཟུང་འཇུག་དབུ་མའི་ལམ། །
།མཐའ་བྲལ་སེམས་ཀྱི་ཆོས་ཉིད་རྟོགས་པར་ཤོག

།ཅི་གསུངས་ཏེ། འཁོར་འདས་ཐམས་ཅད་སེམས་ཡིན་ན་སེམས་དེ་
བདེན་གྲུབ་ཏུ་ཡོད་དམ་ཞེ་ན། བདེན་གྲུབ་ཏུ་ཡོད་པ་ལྟ་ཅི་སྟོས་
བདེན་བརྫུན་གང་གི་ཕྱོགས་དོར་ཡང་ཡོད་པ་མ་ཡིན་ཏེ། རྒྱལ་བ་
ཐམས་ཅད་མཁྱེན་པའི་ཡེ་ཤེས་ཀྱིས་ཀྱང་མ་གཟིགས་མི་གཟིགས་
གཟིགས་པར་མི་འགྱུར་གསུངས་པའི་ཕྱིར། ཨོ་ན་ཅང་མེད་བེམ་སྟོང་
ནས་མཁའ་ལྟ་བུར་བསྟབས་ཞེ་ན། དེ་ལྟར་དུ་འང་མི་བལྟ་སྟེ་སེམས་
རང་བཞིན་གྱིས་དག་པའི་ཁམས་དེ་མེད་ན་འཁོར་འདས་ཀྱི་སྣང་
བ་ཀུན་རྫོབ་ཚལ་དུ་འང་འབྱུང་མི་རིགས་པའི་ཕྱིར་མེད་པ་འང་མ་
ཡིན་ཏེ། འཁོར་བར་འཁྱལ་གཞི་དང་མྱང་འདས་སུ་གྲོལ་གཞི་སྟེ་
འཁོར་འདས་ཀུན་གྱི་གཞི་ཡིན་པའི་ཕྱིར་སྟོབ་དཔོན་སྐྱ་ཞབས་ཀྱིས།

in the pure mind grow clearer. When all stains are purified, all the qualities of the ground manifest, as is taught in the *Mahāyāna Highest Continuum*.[24] You should understand that it is for this reason that as the disciples' mindstreams are gradually purified, they [gradually] see the three kāyas of a buddha.

b) Ascertaining that mind has no intrinsic existence

This has two parts: abandoning extremes of existence/nonexistence and being/nonbeing.

i) Avoiding extremes of existence and nonexistence

11. *It does not exist; even the victors don't see it.*
It doesn't not exist; it's the basis of all samsara and nirvana.
No contradiction; it's the middle way of unity.
May I realize mind's true nature without extremes.

If the whole of samsara and nirvana is the mind, wouldn't that mind be established as truly existing? Never mind being established as truly existent, even discard any sort of validity or falsity, for **it does not exist**. As it says, all **the victors** with their timeless awareness that knows all **don't see it**, have not seen it, and will not see it. Well then, can we view it as being like space, with nothing at all but empty matter? Don't look at it that way either. Because if it were not for mind's naturally pure constituent,[25] it would be unreasonable for all the appearances of samsara and nirvana to arise even conventionally. So **it doesn't not exist**, because **it is the basis of all samsara and nirvana**—the basis of delusion in samsara and the basis of liberation in nirvana. Master Nāgārjuna said,

ཁམས་ཡོད་ན་ནི་ལས་བྱས་པས། །ས་ལེ་སྦྲམ་དག་མཐོང་བར་འགྱུར། །ཁམས་མེད་ན་ནི་ལས་བྱང་ཀྱང་། །ངལ་བ་འབའ་ཞིག་སྐྱེད་པར་ཟད། །ཅེས་གསུངས་སོ། །དེ་ན་གཞི་གཅིག་ལ་ཡོད་མེད་གཉིས་འགལ་ལོ། །ཞི་ན། འགལ་བ་འདུ་བཞང་ཡིན་ཏེ་ཡོད་མེད་གཉིས་བཀག་པ་ལས་བསྒྲུབ་པ་མ་ཡིན་པའི་ཕྱིར། དེས་ན་ཡོད་མེད་སྟོང་མི་སྟོང་སོགས་གང་དུའང་བརྫོང་མི་རུས་ལ་གང་དུའང་མི་གནས་ཤིང་མཐའ་བྲལ་དེ་ལ་བྲང་འཇུག་རབ་ཏུ་མི་གནས་པའི་དབུ་མའི་ལམ་ཞེས་ཐ་སྙད་ཙམ་དུ་གདགས་པ་ཡིན་པས་དེ་ལྟ་བུའི་མཐའ་བྲལ་སེམས་ཀྱི་ཆོས་ཉིད་སྟོས་པ་ཀུན་བྲལ་ཉིད་རྟོགས་པར་ཤོག་ཅིག་ཅེས་པའོ། །

གཉིས་པ་ཡིན་མིན་གྱི་མཐའ་སྤོང་བ་ནི།

འདི་ཡིན་ཞེས་པ་གང་གིས་མཚོན་པ་མེད། །འདི་མིན་ཞེས་བྱ་གང་གིས་བཀག་པ་མེད། །བློ་ལས་འདས་པའི་ཆོས་ཉིད་འདུས་མ་བྱས། །ཡང་དག་དོན་གྱི་མཐའ་ནི་ངེས་པར་ཤོག

།ཅེས་གསུངས་ཏེ། འདིའི་དོན་སྤྱིར་ཡོད་མེད་ཀྱི་མཐའ་བཀག་པས་ཀུང་ཤེས་མོད། རང་བཞིན་མཐའ་བྲལ་དེ་ལ་སྟོང་ཉིད་སྐྱེ་མེད་བདེ་ཆེན་ཡེ་ཤེས་སོགས་མིང་སྣན་དགུས་འདི་ལྟར་ཡིན་ནོ་ཞེས་པ་དཔེ་ཚིག་གང་གིས་ཀྱང་མཚོན་པ་མེད་ཅིད། འདི་ནི་འདི་ལྟར་མིན་ནོ་མེད་དོ་ཞེས་བྱ་བའི་དཔེ་ཚིག་གང་གིས་ཀྱང་བཀག་པ་བྱུར་མེད་དེ་མཚོན་བྱའི་ཆོས་དང་དགག་བསྒྲུབ་ཀྱི་གཞི་མ་གྲུབ་ཅིང་བློའི་སྤྱོད་ཡུལ་ལས་འདས་པའི་ཕྱིར་སྣས་ཀྱང་བརྫོང་མི་རུས་ཏེ།

> If the constituent is present,
> with effort you will see pure gold.
> Without the constituent,
> effort generates nothing but affliction.[26]

But isn't it a contradiction for a single basis to be both existent and nonexistent? It is an internal **contradiction** because it did not establish [something] by refuting both existence and nonexistence. Therefore, you cannot say anything at all, such as existence, nonexistence, empty, not empty, and so forth, and since there is no traction anywhere, it is free of extremes—so **it is** called the "**middle way** path **of** total nonabiding **unity**."[27] Since that is a mere designation, we aspire to **realize** the **true nature** of **mind without extremes**,[28] actual freedom from all embellishment.

ii) Avoiding extremes of being and nonbeing

12. *To say "this is" doesn't indicate anything.*
To say "this is not" doesn't refute anything.
Unformed true nature defies the intellect.
May I gain certainty in the range of genuine reality.

Certainly you can comprehend the meaning here through the previous refutation of the extremes of existence and nonexistence. There are many sweet-sounding names for that intrinsic nature free of extremes that you can use **to say** "**it is** like **this**," such as "emptiness," "unborn," "great bliss," "timeless awareness," and so forth. But these metaphorical words **do not indicate anything. To say** "**this is not** like this" and use metaphorical words also **does not refute anything.** That is because

མདོ་ལས། ཡང་དག་ཉིད་དུ་གཉིས་མེད་དེ། །དེ་ནི་སྟོངས་པ་མེད་པ་
ཡིན། །འཇིག་རྟེན་དཔལ་གྱིས་ནི་ཡང་དག་རིག །རྒྱལ་བའི་སྲས་པོ་མི་
སྐྱ་བཞུགས། །ཞིས་འབྱུང་བའི་ཕྱིར་རོ། འདས་དེ་ནི་ཚོ་ས་ཐམས་ཅད་
ཀྱི་ཚོས་ཉིད་ཡིན་ཅིང་འདུས་མ་བྱས་པའི་ཕྱིར་སྟོས་པའི་རྒྱུན་གང་
གིས་ཀྱང་འགྱུར་བ་མེད་པའི་དེ་བཞིན་ཉིད་དང་། མཚན་མ་མེད་པ་
དང་། དོན་དམ་དང་། ཚོས་དབྱིངས་དང་། ཡང་དག་པའི་མཐའ་ཞིས་
རྣམ་གྲངས་དུ་མས་བསྟན་པའི་གནས་ལུགས་སྟོང་ཉིད་ཀྱི་དོན་ནི་
སོམ་ཉི་མེད་པའི་ངེས་པ་རྙེད་པར་ཟོག་ཅིག་ཅེས་པའོ། །འདིར་ཀུན་
མཁྱེན་སི་ཏུའི་གསུང་སྙིང་པོར་བསྲུས་ཏེ་གོ་སླ་བར་བཀོད་པ་ཡིན་
ལ། འདིའི་དོན་མཚམ་མེད་དྲགས་པོའི་གསུང་གསང་གིས་གསལ་
བར་འཆད་དུ་འང་ཡོད་དོ། །

གསུམ་པ་སྟོང་དང་རྟེན་འབྱུང་ཟུང་འཇུག་མི་འགལ་བ་ནི།

འདི་ཉིད་མ་རྟོགས་འཁོར་བའི་རྒྱུ་མཚོར་འཁོར། །འདི་ཉིད་རྟོགས་
ན་སངས་རྒྱས་གཞན་ན་མེད། །ཐམས་ཅད་འདི་ཡིན་འདི་མིན་གང་
ཡང་མེད། །ཚོས་ཉིད་ཀུན་གཞིའི་མཚང་ནི་རིག་པར་ཟོག

།ཅེས་གསུངས་ཏེ། དེས་ན་གནས་ལུགས་སེམས་ཀྱི་གསང་འདི་ཉིད་
མ་རྟོགས་པ་ལས་ལུགས་འབྱུང་རྟེན་བྲེལ་གྱིས་འཁོར་བའི་རྒྱུ་མཚོར་

the phenomena that are indicated and the bases of refutation and affirmation are not established, so it **defies** the realm of **the intellect**. It cannot even be expressed by sound. It says in a sutra:

> The nonduality of the genuine state
> is without embellishment.
> When Mañjuśrī inquired about it,
> the bodhisattva sat silently.[29]

Therefore it transcends the intellect because it is the **true nature** (*dharmatā*) of all phenomena (*dharma*) and therefore **is unformed**, not subject to any conditions of embellishment. Unchanging suchness, no characteristics, ultimate reality, realm of phenomena, **range of genuine reality**—these many synonyms are used to present the abiding nature, the meaning of emptiness. We aspire to gain certainty without doubt.

Here, all-knowing Situ[30] has presented an abridged essence of his teachings for easy comprehension. Its meaning was also clearly explicated in the secret teachings of the Unequalled Dakpo (Gampopa).

c) The unity of emptiness and interdependence is not contradictory

13. *Not to realize this is to flounder in samsara's ocean.*
To realize it is nothing other than buddhahood.
Being all, "this is it" and "this is not it" mean nothing at all.
May I awaken to the true nature hidden in the all-ground.

Not to realize this, the abiding nature, the secret of the mind, is to **flounder in the ocean of samsara** through

འབོར་བ་ཡིན་ལ། འདི་ཉིད་རྟོགས་ན་ལུགས་སྟོག་རྟེན་འབྲེལ་གྱིས་
འཚང་རྒྱ་བ་ཡིན་པས་སངས་རྒྱས་དེ་འང་གནས་ལུགས་ཀྱི་དོན་
འདི་ལས་གཞན་ལོགས་ཤིག་ན་མེད་ཅིང་། གནས་ལུགས་དེ་བཞིན་
ཉིད་སངས་རྒྱས་ཀྱི་རང་བཞིན་འདིས་ཆོས་ཐམས་ཅད་ལ་ཡེ་ནས་
ཁྱབ་པས་ཐམས་ཅད་འདི་ཡིན་ལ། འདི་མིན་པའི་ཆོས་ཤིག་གང་དུ་
བཙལ་ཡང་རྙེད་པ་མེད་དེ། ཆོས་རྣམས་རྟེན་འབྱུང་ཡིན་པའི་རྒྱུན་
མཚན་གྱིས་སྟོང་ཉིད་དུ་གོ་བར་ནུས་ཏེ་སྟོང་ཉིད་མ་ཡིན་ན་རྟེན་
འབྱུང་མི་རུང་བའི་ཕྱིར། ཀླུ་སྒྲུབ་ཞབས་ཀྱིས། རྟེན་ཅིང་འབྲེལ་འབྱུང་
མ་ཡིན་པའི། །ཆོས་འགའ་ཡོད་པ་མ་ཡིན་ལ། །འདི་ཕྱིར་སྟོང་ཉིད་
མ་ཡིན་པའི། །ཆོས་འགར་ཡོད་པ་མ་ཡིན་ནོ། །ཞེས་སོགས་རྒྱ་ཆེར་
གསུངས་པ་ལྟར་སྣང་བ་རྟེན་འབྱུང་གི་ངོ་བོ་སྟོང་པ་ཉིད་ཀྱི་ཕྱིར་
ཟུང་དུ་འཇུག་པ་སྟེ། དེ་ལྟར་ཆོས་ཐམས་ཅད་ཀྱི་ཆོས་ཉིད་དེ་བཞིན་
ཉིད་ཀུན་གཞི་དང་ལུགས་དགེ་བ་ཞེས་བྱ་བའི་གནད་མཚང་ཇི་ལྟ་
བ་བཞིན་དུ་ནི་རིག་པར་ཤོག་ཅིག་ཅེས་པའོ། །

བཞི་པ་དེ་ལྟར་བཀྲགས་པས་གཞི་རྩ་ཆོད་པར་སྟོན་པ་ནི།

རླུང་ཡང་སེམས་ལ་སྟོང་ཡང་སེམས་ཡིན་ཏེ། །རྟོགས་ཀྱང་སེམས་ལ་
འཁྲུལ་ཡང་རང་གི་སེམས། །སྐྱེས་ཀྱང་སེམས་ལ་འགག་ཀྱང་སེམས་
ཡིན་པས། །སྣ་འདོགས་ཐམས་ཅད་སེམས་ལ་ཆོད་པར་ཤོག

interdependent origination operating in progressive order. **To realize it** is **buddhahood** due to interdependent origination operating in reverse order. Therefore, that buddhahood is **nothing other than** this very meaning of the abiding nature. The abiding nature, suchness, the intrinsic nature of a buddha, pervades all phenomena since forever. Therefore, **all is this**. However much you search, you cannot find a single phenomenon that **is not this**. All phenomena are interdependently arisen. For that reason, we can understand emptiness; for if there were no emptiness, interdependent origination would make no sense. Noble Nāgārjuna said,

> There do not exist any phenomena
> that do not originate interdependently.
> Therefore, there do not exist any phenomena
> that are not emptiness.[31]

Likewise, it is explained at length that since emptiness is the essence of the interdependent origination of appearance, they are a unified pair. In this way, the **true nature** of all phenomena, the suchness, abides intrinsically within **the all-ground** and is called "virtue." We aspire to **awaken to** this inner **hidden nature** just as it is.

d) The aspiration to cut through the basic root by such examination

14. *As appearance is mind, so too emptiness is mind.*
As realization is mind, delusion is also one's mind.
As birth is mind, so is cessation the mind.
May I sever all the impositions of mind.

།ཅེས་གསུངས་ཏེ། མདོར་ན་སྣང་སྟོང་ཆོག་འབྱལ་སྐྱེ་འགག་རྣམས་
སྤྲ་སྐྱོས་པའི་རྒྱུན་མཚན་དེ་དག་ཇེས་པའི་སྐྱོ་ནས་རང་བཞིན་
མེད་པར་གཏན་ལ་ཕབ་པ་གནས་ལུགས་ཀྱི་སྐྱོ་འདོགས་ཐམས་ཅད་
སེམས་ལ་ཆོད་པར་ཤོག་ཅེས་སམ། མདོར་ན་ཀུན་རྫོབ་ཏུ་སྣང་བ་
ཡང་སེམས་ཀྱི་འབྱུལ་བ་ཡིན་ལ་དོན་དམ་སྟོང་པ་ཡང་སེམས་ཀྱི་
གནས་ལུགས་ཡིན་ཏེ། དེ་ཉིད་ཆོགས་ནས་སངས་རྒྱས་ཀྱང་དག་པའི་
སེམས་ཉིད་ཡིན་ལ་འབྱུལ་ཏེ་འཁོར་བར་འཁྱམས་ན་ཡདཿ རང་གི་
མ་དག་པའི་སེམས་སྣང་ཡིན་པའི་ཕྱིར་དེས་ན་སེམས་རྒྱུད་མར་སྐྱེས་
ཏེ་སྐྱིད་པར་འཁྱམས་ཀྱང་སེམས་ཡིན་ལ་སོ་སོར་བཏགས་འགོག་
གིས་འགགས་ཏེ་ཞི་བ་ཐོབ་ཀྱང་སེམས་ཡིན་པས་བདེན་གཉིས་
འཁོར་འདས་སྲིད་ཞི་སོགས་ཐམས་ཅད་སེམས་ཏུ་བཅུས་ཏུ་མེད་
གཉིས་ལས་མ་འདས་ཤིང་། དེའང་སྟོང་པ་གཞི་མེད་རྩ་བྲལ་མཐའ་
གང་དུའང་མི་གནས་པས་བློ་འདས་ཉིད་ཏུ་ངེས་པའི་སྐྱོ་འདོགས་
ཐམས་ཅད་སེམས་ལ་ཆོད་ནས་དེ་ཉིད་མངོན་ཏུ་བྱ་ཐབས་གཟུང་
འཛིན་གྱི་དྲི་མ་སྤྱོང་ཕྱིར་སྐྱོམ་པ་ཐམས་ཞེན་ལ་འབད་པར་ཤོག་
ཅེས་ལྤ་བ་ལ་ཇེས་པ་ཉེད་ནས་སྐྱོམ་པ་ལ་འཇུག་པར་མཚམས་སྦྱར་
བ་སྟེ། རྒྱུད་ལས། རིན་ཆེན་སེམས་ལས་ཕྱིར་གྱུར་པའི། །སངས་རྒྱས་
མེད་ཅིང་སེམས་ཅན་མེད། །ཅེས་དང་། གྲུབ་པའི་སྐྱི་མེས་ས་ར་ད་
པས།

In brief, may we cut through all superimpositions of appearance and emptiness, realization and delusion, birth and cessation, imposed on the abiding nature by ascertaining their lack of intrinsic nature and by gaining the certainty in the reasons presented previously.

Or, in brief, **as** conventional **appearance is** also the delusion of the **mind, so too** the **emptiness** of ultimate reality **is mind**'s abiding nature. Once there is **realization** of that very truth, even buddha is pure **mind** itself. **As** that is [obscured by] **delusion,** one wanders in cyclic existence. However, since that is the appearance of **one's** impure **mind**, the mental continuum takes **birth** in a mother and wanders in existence. However, this is also mind and may be stopped by the **cessation** from discriminating analysis and peace gained, which too **is mind**. Therefore all designations such as the two truths, samsara and nirvana, existence and peace, and so forth do not transcend the two aspects of stained or stainless mind. Baseless and rootless emptiness does not exist in any extreme whatsoever. With the certitude in that state beyond intellect, **may I sever all the superimpositions** [by realizing them as] the **mind**. Since the method to manifest that is to purify the stains of subject–object dualism, we aspire to endeavor in the practice of meditation. This is the juncture of entering into meditation once one has gained certainty in the view. It says in a tantra:

> Outside of the precious mind
> there are no buddhas or sentient beings.[32]

There are vast teachings on this, such as by our ancestor, the adept Saraha:

ཤེས་ཉིད་གཅིག་པུ་ཀུན་གྱི་ས་བོན་ཏེ། །གང་ལས་སྲིད་དང་མྱང་
འདས་འཕྲོ་བ། །འདོད་པའི་འབྲས་བུ་སྟེར་བར་བྱེད་པ་ཡི།
།ཡིད་བཞིན་ནོར་འདྲའི་སེམས་ལ་ཕྱག་འཚལ་ལོ། །ཞེས་སོགས་རྒྱ་
ཆེར་གསུངས་པའི་ཕྱིར་རོ། །

གཞིས་པ་སྟོམ་པས་ཉམས་སུ་ལེན་ཚུལ་ལ། བསྟན། བཤད་གཞིས་
ལས། དང་པོ་མདོར་བསྟན་པ་ནི།

བློས་བྱས་ཚོལ་བའི་སྟོམ་གྱིས་མ་བསླད་ཅིང་། །ཐ་མལ་འདུ་འཛིའི་
རྐྱང་གིས་མ་བསྐྱོད་པར། །མ་བཅོས་གཉུག་མར་རང་བབས་འཇོག་
ཤེས་པའི། །སེམས་དོན་ཉམས་ལེན་མཁས་ཤིང་སྐྱོང་བར་ཤོག

།ཅེས་གསུངས་ཏེ། ཀུན་མཁྱེན་སྱི་ཏུས་འདིའི་ཚིག་ཁང་གཞིས་པ་
ཐོག་མར་བྱས་ན་བཤད་བདེ་བར་གསུངས་པ་ལྟར། དང་པོ་སྟོམ་ལ་
འཇུག་པའི་ཚུལ་མཚན་ཉུན་གྱི་བླ་མ་ཚུལ་བཞིན་བསྟེན་པའི་སྐལ་
ལྡན་གྱི་སྟོབ་མ་ནིས། ཐོག་མར་ཕྱིམ་དང་དག་གཉིན་ནོར་རྫས་རྙེད་
བཀུར་སོགས་འཇིག་རྟེན་ཚོས་བཀྱུད་ལ་ཞེན་པའི་ཚགས་སྤང་མ་
སྤང་ན་ཐར་པ་ལྟ་ཅི་སྙོས་མཐོ་རིས་ཀྱང་མི་འཐོབ་པས་སྟོ་གསུམ་
འཇིག་རྟེན་ཐ་མལ་པའི་སྐྱོད་པ་འདུ་འཛིའི་རྐྱང་གིས་མ་བསྐྱོད

Mind itself is the single seed of all,
from which existence and nirvana emanate.
Homage to mind, like a wish-fulfilling gem
that grants the gift of the desired fruit.[33]

B) How to take into experience through meditation
This has two parts, a brief presentation and an explanation.

1) Brief presentation

15. *Unspoiled by meditation with mind-made effort,*
unmoved by the winds of everyday affairs,
knowing how to fall naturally in the uncontrived innate state;
may I skillfully maintain the practice of mind's meaning.

The all-knowing Situ said that it is better to explain this verse
if the second line comes first. In keeping with that, first we
will discuss the way to enter into meditation. Those who
attend an authentic guru correctly are fortunate disciples.
But if right from the start they do not abandon attraction
and aversion that clings to a household and the eight worldly
concerns—including friend and foe, property and wealth,
honor and gain—they will not even attain higher states, let
alone emancipation. Therefore, stay in a remote place and
practice **unmoved by the winds of everyday affairs** and
worldly activities of the three doors. Train with the common,
uncommon, and special preliminaries, positively blending
them with your very being and not just according to duration
of time or accumulation of repetitions. That way, mind will
turn toward Dharma, Dharma will become the path, and the

པར་དབེན་པའི་གནས་སུ། ཕྱུན་མོང་དང་ཕྱུན་མིན་དང་བྱུད་པར་
གྱི་སྟོན་འགྲོ་རྣམས་དུས་གྲངས་ཚམ་མིན་པར་རང་རྒྱུད་ལ་འདྲེས་
ཏེས་པ་སྐྱངས་པས་བློ་ཚོས་དང་ཚོས་ལམ་དུ་འགྲོ་ཞིང་ཕྱག་ཆེན་གྱི་
ཡེ་ཤེས་ཚུལ་མེད་དུ་སྐྱེ་བའི་རྟེན་འབྲེལ་ལེགས་པར་བསྒྲིགས་ནས།
བར་དུ་མཉམ་པར་འཇོག་ཆུལ་ལས་གནད་ཆུལ་བཞིན་བཅས་ནས་
རྒྱུང་རོ་བསལ། སེམས་གནད་རང་གི་བློ་བྱ་པའི་གསལ་བ་དང་
སྟོང་པ་སོགས་ལེགས་ལེགས་ལྱ་བུའི་ཚུལ་བའི་སྣོམ་གྱིས་མ་བསླད་
ཅིད། དཔལ་ས་ར་ཏྱས། འདི་ལྟར་དུས་གསུམ་རྣམ་པ་ཐམས་ཅད་
དུ། །ཡིད་ལ་བྱར་མེད་མ་བྲལ་གཏུག་མའི་ངང་། །དེ་ཉིད་སྐྱོང་ལ་
སྣོམ་ཞེས་ཐ་སྙད་གདགས། །ཞེས་གསུངས་པ་ལྟར་བཀའ་བརྒྱུད་གོང་
མ་རྣམས་ཀྱི་ཞལ་ནས། འདྲས་པའི་རྟེས་མི་གཅད། མ་འོངས་པའི་
མདུན་མི་བསུ། ད་ལྟར་གྱི་ཤེས་པ་བཟོ་བཅོས་མེད་པར་རང་བབས་
སུ་འཇོག་གསུངས་པ་ལྟར་མ་བཅོས་གཏུག་མའི་ངང་ལ་རང་བབས་
སུ་འཇོག་ཤེས་པའི་སེམས་དོན་ཉམས་སུ་ལེན་པའི་མན་ངག་གི་
གནད་ལ་སགས་ཤིང་བྱིང་རྒོད་བསལ་བ། གོལ་ས་གཅོད་པ། བོགས་
འདོན་པ་རྣམས་ཀྱང་ཇི་བཞིན་ཤེས་པའི་སྒོ་ནས་འབྲས་བུའི་ཕྱག་
ཆེན་མཆོན་དུ་མ་གྱུར་གྱི་བར་དུ་རྒྱུན་བསྐྱངས་ཏེ་སྐྱོང་བར་བུས་
པའི་སྐལ་པ་དང་ལྡན་པར་ཤོག་ཅིག་ཅེས་པའོ། །ཅི་ཐོག་མ་ཉིད་
ནས་བཟོ་མེད་དུ་སྐྱོང་བ་ཉིད་ལ་འཇུག་གམ་ཞེ་ན། འཇུག་པར་ནུས་
ན་ཆེས་ལེགས་ཤིང་གང་ཟག་གི་དབང་པོའི་རིམ་པས་མ་ནུས་ན།
འཕགས་པ་ཀླུས། དམིགས་པ་དག་ལ་བརྟེན་ནས་ནི། །དམིགས་མེད་
པ་ཉིད་རབ་ཏུ་སྐྱེ། །

interdependent connections are set into motion for the timeless awareness of mahāmudrā to arise effortlessly.

In the middle, (until then), practice clearing away the
dead air according to the vital points from the teachings on
the way of entering equipoise. For the vital points of mind,
remain **unspoiled by meditation with effort** that is like being
impressed by **mind-made** clarity and emptiness and so forth,
and follow glorious Saraha's teaching:

> In this way, during all the three times,
> maintain the innate state free of mental engagement;
> this is what is meant by the term "meditation."[34]

Just so, the Kagyü masters of the past all said, "Do not get
stuck in the past, do not go out to greet the future, fall naturally in the wakefulness of the present moment without arti-
fice or contrivance." Accordingly, **know how to fall naturally
in the uncontrived innate state** with **skill** in the vital points
of the esoteric instructions concerning the practice of **mind's
meaning**. By means of the accurate knowledge of how to
eliminate dullness and agitation, cutting off deviations, and
employing the enhancements, you continue to **maintain the
practice** until the actualization of the result: mahāmudrā. We
aspire to become fortunate ones with that ability.

You may wonder whether anyone can maintain that unfab-
ricated state right from the very beginning. Well, if one can, all
the better. But since there are gradations in people's faculties,
you may not have that ability. Then, as [Maitreyanātha] said,

> Through relying on reference points,
> the nonreferential itself will fully emerge.[35]

ཞེས་གསུངས་པ་ལྟར་སེམས་འཛིན་དམིགས་རྟེན་ཏི་ལྟར་རིགས་པ་
ལས་རིམ་པར་བསླབ་བོ། །

གཉིས་པ་རྒྱས་བཤད་ལ་གསུམ། ཞི་ལྷག་གི་རྣལ་འབྱོར། ཕྱམས་
ཆོགས་སྐྱེ་ཚུལ། བཅུ་སྟོང་བྱུང་འཇུག་གོ །དང་པོ་ལའང་གསུམ། ཞི་
གནས། ལྷག་མཐོང་། བྱུང་འཇུག་གོ །དང་པོ་ ཞི་གནས་ དི།

ཕྱ་རགས་ཆོག་པའི་ཙ་རྣབས་རང་སར་ཞི། །གཡོ་མེད་སེམས་ཀྱི་རྒྱུ་
པོ་དང་གིས་གནས། །ཕྱིང་རྒྱགས་ཆོག་པའི་ཏི་མ་དང་བྲལ་བའི། །ཞི་
གནས་རྒྱུ་མཚོ་མི་གཡོ་བརྟན་པར་ཤོག།

།ཅེས་གསུངས་ཏེ། མཇོད་ལས་དཔྱོད་པ་དང་ཆོག་པ་ལ་ཕྱ་རགས་
སུ་བཤད་མོད་འདིར་མན་ངག་ཏུ་ཡུལ་ལ་འཇུག་པའི་ཆོག་དཔྱོད་
མཇོན་གྱུར་མི་ཚོར་བའི་ཕྱ་བ་དང་། དེ་ཚོར་བའི་རགས་པ་སྟེ་སེམས་
བྱུང་ཆོག་པའི་དབང་རྣབས་དེ་ཆེད་དུ་བཀགག་པ་མ་ཡིན་པ་དང་
གིས་འགགས་པས་རང་སར་ཞི་གནས་གཡོ་བ་མེད་པར་སེམས་ཀྱི་
རྒྱུ་པོ་དེ་ཉིད་དང་གིས་གནས་ཤིང་། ཕྱིང་རྒྱགས་སོགས་བསམ་གཏན་
གྱི་སྒྲིབ་པ་ཕྱིང་ཆོག་པའི་ཏི་མ་ཐམས་ཅད་དང་བྲལ་བའི་ཞི་གནས་
ཀྱི་རྒྱུ་མཚོ་རྒྱེན་གང་གིས་ཀྱང་མི་གཡོ་བར་བཅན་པ་མཐར་ཕྱིན་
པར་ཤོག་ཅིག་ཅེས་པའོ། །བསམ་གཏན་གྱི་སྒྲིབ་པ་ལྷ་ཞི། རྒྱུ་ཞབས་
ཀྱི་བཉིས་སྒྲིང་ལས་གསུངས་པ་ལྟར། ཡུལ་སྣ་ཚོགས་ལ་ཆོག་པ་
འཛོ་བའི་རྟོད་པ་དང་། མི་རིགས་པ་བྱས་པ་ལ་འགྱོད་པ་གཉིས་ཀྱིས་

In that way, train successively with whatever reference supports are suitable for gaining focused attention.

2) Extensive explanation
This has three parts: the yogas of calm abiding and higher insight, the way experience and realization arise, and the unity of love and emptiness.

a) Calm abiding and higher insight

i) Calm abiding

16. *The waves of subtle and coarse thoughts subside in themselves.*
The river of unmoved mind abides within itself.
Free of the murky stains of dullness and darkness,
may the unmoving ocean of calm abiding be steady.

Of course there are explanations of subtle and coarse discriminating concepts in the *Abhidharma*, but here we are concerned with the esoteric instructions. **Thoughts** and discriminations apprehending objective reality that are not evident or felt **are subtle** and those that are felt are **coarse**. Without blocking **the waves** of mental events and concepts on purpose, allow them to cease from within and **subside in themselves**. Then **the** broad **river of mind** will **abide without moving within** this **itself, free of** all **the stains** of drifting **murky** sediment. We aspire to reach the **ocean of calm abiding, steady and unmoved** by any conditions whatsoever, such as the **dullness and darkness** that obscure meditative **stability**.

སེམས་ཉི་བར་གནས་པའི་གེགས་བྱེད། གཉེད་སེམས་ཀྱིས་བདེ་བར་
གནས་པའི་གེགས་བྱེད། སེམས་འཕྱིབས་པའི་བྱིང་བ་དང་དེ་བས་
ཆེར་བྱིང་བའི་རྨུགས་པ་དང་གཉིད་དེ་གསུམ་གྱིས་གསལ་བར་
གནས་པའི་གེགས་བྱེད། ཡོ་བྱད་དང་སེམས་ཅན་ལ་ཆགས་པའི་
འདོད་འདུན་གྱིས་ལས་རུང་དུ་གནས་པའི་གེགས་བྱེད། འདི་སྐྲོན་
ཡིན་ནམ་མིན་སྣམ་པ་སོགས་ཏེ་ཆོམ་གྱིས་ཆེ་གཅིག་པར་གནས་
པའི་གེགས་བྱེད་པའོ། །ལྟ་པོ་དེ་འང་བརྟུ་ན། བྱིང་རྟོད་གཉིས་སུ་འདུ་
ལ་དེ་དག་སེལ་ཐབས་སོ་སོའི་གཉེན་པོ་བརྟེན་པ་དང་། གཙོ་བོར་
བྱིང་རྟོད་ཀྱི་རང་པོ་བལྟ་ཞིང་དེའི་ངོ་བོར་མ་བཅོས་པར་འཇོག་པ་
ཉིད་ཟབ་པར་གསུངས། སྒྱིར་ཉེས་པ་ལྔ་སྤོང་ཕྱིར་འདུ་བྱེད་བརྒྱད་
བརྟེན་པ་དང་། སེམས་དགུ་ལ་མཉམ་བཞག་གྲུབ་ནས་བསམ་གཏན་
ཆམས་སྐྱབ་པའི་ཚུལ་ཉེས་ནའང་ལེགས་སོ། །

གཉིས་པ་ལྷག་མཐོང་ལ་གཉིས། དངོས་དང་། ཞི་ཆུ་གཅོད་པའོ།
།དང་པོ་ ་དངོས་ ་ ནི།

བསྒྱར་མེད་སེམས་ལ་ཡང་ཡང་བསྒྱས་པའི་ཆོ། །མཐོང་མེད་དོན་ནི་
ཏེ་བཞིན་ལྷག་གིར་མཐོང་། །ཡིན་མིན་དོན་ལ་ཐེ་ཚོམ་ཆོད་པ་ཉིད།
།འཁྲུལ་མེད་རང་རོ་རང་གིས་ཤེས་པར་ཤོག

The five obscurations of meditative stability according to Venerable Nāgārjuna in *Letter to a Friend*[36] are: (1) Agitation of the thoughts emanating to various objects and regret over inappropriate actions, both of which hinder the calm abiding of mind. (2) Malice hinders abiding in happiness. (3) Dullness of a heavy mind, and darkness that is even duller than that, and sleep; these three hinder abiding in clarity. (4) Desirous attachment to beings or things hinders effective abiding. (5) Doubts such as whether this is meditation or is not meditation hinder the abiding in undivided attention.

To condense those five, they can be included in two: dullness and agitation. You should rely on the antidotes of the specific methods to clear them up. The main thing is to look at the actual aspect of dullness and agitation and then settle in their essence without contrivance. This itself is said to be the most profound. In general, in order to eliminate these five flaws, it is also good to know the way to accomplish all meditative stability by relying on the eight remedies[37] and achieve equipoise by means of the nine methods of mental abiding.[38]

ii) Higher insight
This has two parts: the main part and severing the ground-root of peace.

(A) The main part, higher insight

17. *When you look again and again for imperceptible mind,*
you see distinctly the meaning of not seeing, just as it is.
Severing doubts about the meaning of being and nonbeing,
may I know my own unmistakable nature.

།ཅེས་གསུངས་ཏེ། བསྐུ་བའི་ཡུལ་ལས་འདས་པས་བསྐུ་བྱར་མེད་
པའི་སེམས་ཀྱི་གནས་ལུགས་དེ་ཉིད་ལ་མ་ཨཐལ་པར་བཞག་ཅིང་བླ་
མའི་མན་ངག་དང་སྦྱོར་བྱུང་གི་ཤེས་རབ་ཀྱི་མིག་གིས་ཡང་དང་
ཡང་དུ་བལྟས་པ་དེའི་ཚེ་མཐོང་བྱའི་དངོས་པོ་མེད་ཕྱིར་མཐོང་བ་
དང་བྲལ་བའི་དོན་དེ་ཉིད་ནི་ཇི་ལྟ་བ་བཞིན་ལྷག་གེར་མཐོང་བས་
ཡིན་མིན་ཡོད་མེད་སོགས་གནས་ལུགས་ཀྱི་དོན་དེ་ལ་སྒྲོ་སྐུར་དང་
བྱེ་ཚོམ་ཚོད་པ་དེ་ཉིད་འཁྲུལ་བ་མེད་པའི་རང་རོ་རང་གིས་ཤེས་
པའི་ཚུལ་དུ་ལྷག་མཐོང་གི་ཡེ་ཤེས་སྐྱེས་ནས་ལྷན་སྐྱེས་ཕྱག་རྒྱ་ཆེན་
པོ་མཛོན་དུ་འགྱུར་བར་ཕོག་ཅིག་ཅེས་པའོ། །དེའང་བསམ་པ་དང་།
སྦྱོམ་པ་དང་། ལྟ་བ་དང་། ཤེས་པ་དང་། མཐོང་བ་དང་། སྱོང་བ་ལ་
སོགས་པའི་མཚན་མ་ཐམས་ཅད་དང་བྲལ་བའི་གནས་ལུགས་ཤེས་
པ་ལ་དེ་དང་དེར་བཏགས་པ་ཙམ་སྟེ། ཆད་སྟོང་མེད་དགག་ཙམ་
ལ་ཡང་དག་པའི་དོན་དུ་བཟུང་བ་བཟས་པོའི་སྟོང་ཉིད་དུ་བཞད་པ་
སོགས་མ་རིག་པའི་སྒྲིབ་གཡོག་དང་བྲལ་བས་རང་རིག་པ་དང་། སྒྲོ་
འདོགས་དང་བྱེ་ཚོམ་ལ་སོགས་པ་ཆོད་པས་ཐེས་པ་རྙེད་པ་དང་། མི་
བདེ་བའི་རྒྱལ་པར་ཏོག་པའི་འགྱུར་བ་ཐམས་ཅད་སྱངས་པས་བདེ་
བ་ཆེན་པོར་འཇོག་པ་སོགས་ཤེས་དགོས་པར་གསུངས་སོ། །

གཉིས་པ་གཞི་རྩ་གཅོད་པ་ནི།

ཡུལ་ལ་བལྟས་པས་ཡུལ་མེད་སེམས་སུ་མཐོང་། །སེམས་ལ་བལྟས་
པས་སེམས་མེད་རོ་བོས་སྟོང་། །གཉིས་ལ་བལྟས་པས་གཉིས་འཛིན་
རང་སར་གྲོལ། །

Since the mind is beyond being a viewable object, rest in equipoise in the abiding nature of the very mind that is **not** something to **perceive. When you look again and again** with the eye of knowledge that comes from the guru's esoteric instructions and your own meditation, because no actual thing is there to be seen, at that time **you see distinctly** (*lhag ger mthong*; Skt. *vipaśyanā*) **the meaning** of the lack of **seeing** itself, **just as it is**. Through that insight, you **sever doubts** and superimpositions or denials **about the meaning of** the abiding nature, such as whether it is **being or nonbeing**, existent or nonexistent, and so forth. We aspire to develop the timeless awareness of higher insight and actualize innate mahāmudrā in that way of **unmistakably knowing one's own nature** oneself.

This knowledge of the abiding nature is free of all characteristics—such as contemplation, meditation, view, knowledge, insight, experience, and so forth—the mere designations of this or that. It is reflexive awareness because it is free of the veil of ignorance, such as the emptiness of dead matter explained in the nihilistic emptiness of mere negation that is mistaken as the genuine reality, and so forth. It is finding certitude, because it severs superimpositions and doubts. And it is the entrance into great happiness, since it eliminates all unhappy conceptual thoughts. You should know such things.

(B) Severing the underlying root

18. *When you look at objects, there are no objects, you see mind.*
Looking at mind, there is no mind; empty of essence.
Looking at both frees dualistic fixation in its own place.
May I realize lucid clarity, the abiding nature of mind.

།འོད་གསལ་སེམས་ཀྱི་གནས་ལུགས་རྟོགས་པར་ཐོག །ཅེས་གསུངས་
ཏེ། ཡུལ་དྲུག་གང་ཤར་གྱི་སྣང་བ་དེ་དག་གི་སྟེང་དུ་བསླབ་ནས་
མཉམ་པར་བཞག་པས་སྒོམ་བྱུང་གི་ཤེས་རབ་ཀྱིས་ཡུལ་རྣམས་རང་
ངོ་མ་གྲུབ་པར་སེམས་ཚལ་དུ་མཐོང་ཞིང་། དེ་བཞིན་དུ་སེམས་ཉིད་
ཀྱི་རང་ངོ་ལ་བལྟས་ནས་མཉམ་པར་བཞག་པས་སེམས་ཀྱང་གཞི་
མེད་རྩ་བྲལ་ངོ་བོས་སྟོང་པར་རྟོགས་པ་དང་། སྣང་སེམས་གཉིས་
རོ་མཉམ་དུ་མཉམ་པར་བཞག་ལ་བསླབས་པས་ཡུལ་ཡུལ་ཅན་གྱི་
གཉིས་འཛིན་གཉི་མེད་དུ་རང་སར་གྲོལ་ཏེ་རང་བཞིན་གྱིས་སྦྱིབ་
པ་དང་བྲལ་བས་འོད་གསལ་བའི་སེམས་ཀྱི་གནས་ལུགས་ཇི་ལྟ་བ་
བཞིན་རྟོགས་པར་ཐོག་ཅིག་ཅེས་པའོ། །འདི་སྐབས་ཁྲིད་རིམ་རྣམས་
སུ། སྣང་བ་སེམས། སེམས་སྟོང་པ། སྟོང་པ་ལྷུན་གྲུབ། ལྷུན་གྲུབ་རང་
གྲོལ་དུ་ངོ་སྤྲོད་པར་གསུངས་ཏེ། གནས་ལུགས་ཕྱོགས་ཚལ་རྟོགས་
ཀྱང་ཕྱིས་ནས་གཉི་རྩ་གཅོད་པའི་མན་ངག་གིས་ངོ་མ་སྤྲད་ན་ཐེས་
པ་ཉེད་དགའ་བར་གསུངས། དེའི་ཕྱིར་ངོ་འཕྲོད་ནས་ཀྱང་བླ་མའི་
མན་ངག་གི་གནད་གསང་དང་ལྷན་པས་ཚལ་སྒྲུབས་ཏེ་སྐོམ་ལྷ་
ཐོག་ཏུ་སྐྱེལ་དགོས་པར་མཉམ་མེད་བླ་མས་གསུངས་སོ། །དེ་ལྟར་
ཡུལ་དང་སེམས་གཉིས་ཀ་ལ་ལྷ་བར་བྱེད་པ་ནི་ཤེས་རབ་གསུམ་
གྱི་མིག་གིས་ཏེ། དེ་ལས་ཀྱང་ཚོས་ཉེད་ཇི་ལྟ་བ་བཞིན་མཐོན་ནུས་
དུ་མཐལ་བར་བྱེད་པ་ནི་སྐོམ་བྱུང་རྟོག་བྲལ་གྱི་ཤེས་རབ་ཉེད་ཡིན་
པའི་ཕྱིར་བཅྱུད་པ་འདིས་མཉམ་བཞག་ལ་དཔྱད་སྐོམ་མི་མཛད་པ་
ནི་གནད་གསང་བླ་ན་མེད་པར་བཞེད་དོ། །

When you look right **at** the appearances of whichever of the six sense **objects** arises, and then rest in equipoise, with the knowledge that comes from meditation **you** will **see** that there is only **mind; there are no objects** that exist from their own side. Likewise, when you **look** directly **at** the very essence of that **mind** itself and then rest in equipoise, you realize that **there is** also **no** underlying basis or root of **mind**; it is **empty of** an **essence.** Resting in the equipoise of the equal taste of **both** appearance and mind and **looking at** that, the **dualistic fixation** of object and subject is without basis, **free in its own place.** We aspire to realize just as it is **the lucid clarity of the abiding nature of mind**, which is naturally free of obscuration.

The guidance sequence for introducing mind's nature is taught as follows: appearances are introduced as mind, mind as empty, emptiness as spontaneously present, and spontaneous presence as naturally liberated. Even with a generalized realization of the abiding nature, it is said that later you will not gain certitude without the introduction through esoteric instructions of severing the underlying basic root. For that reason, the unequalled guru (Gampopa) said that you must train the energy with the secret vital points of the guru's instructions and convey that directly onto the meditation and view. The eyes of the three wisdoms can produce the view of both object and mind. However, only the nonconceptual wisdom that arises from meditation itself produces the actual encounter of the nature of phenomena or true reality. Therefore, in this lineage, analytic meditation is not done during meditative equipoise. This is considered the unsurpassable secret vital point.

གསུམ་པ་ཟུང་འཇུག་གི་རྣལ་འབྱོར་དེའི་མཚན་གྱི་རྣམ་གྲངས་ནི།

ཡིད་བྱེད་བྲལ་བ་འདི་ནི་ཕྱག་རྒྱ་ཆེ། །མཐའ་དང་བྲལ་བ་དབུ་མ་
ཆེན་པོ་ཡིན། །འདི་ནི་ཀུན་འདུས་རྫོགས་ཆེན་ཞེས་ཀྱང་བྱ། །གཅིག་
ཤེས་ཀུན་དོན་རྟོགས་པའི་གདིང་འཐོབ་ཤོག

།ཅེས་གསུངས་ཏེ། །སྟོན་སྐྱེས་ཡེ་ཤེས་རྗེ་བཞིན་རྟོགས་ནས་མཐའ་
པར་འཛིག་པའི་ཟུང་འཇུག་གི་རྣལ་འབྱོར་དེ་ནི་ཡིད་ལ་བྱེད་པ་
ཐམས་ཅད་དང་བྲལ་བས་ན་འདི་ནི་ཕྱག་རྒྱ་ཆེན་པོ་ཞེས་བྱ་ལ།
མཚན་གྱི་རྣམ་གྲངས་གཞན་ཡང་། སྤྲོས་པའི་མཐའ་ཐམས་ཅད་དང་
བྲལ་བས་ན་དབུ་མ་ཆེན་པོའང་འདི་ཉིད་ཡིན་ལ། འདིར་ནི་ཆོས་
ཀུན་གྱི་རྟོགས་པ་འདུས་པའི་ཕྱིར་རྫོགས་པ་ཆེན་པོ་ཞེས་ཀྱང་བྱ་
སྟེ་དེ་བཞིན་ཉིད་གཅིག་པུ་འདི་ཁོ་ན་ཤེས་པས་ཆོས་རྣམས་ཀུན་
གྱི་དོན་གྱི་གནད་གསང་མ་ལུས་པ་རྟོགས་པས་གདིང་འཐོབ་པར་
ཤོག་ཅིག་ཅེས་པའོ། །རྒྱང་གི་སྐྱས་ཟབ་པ་དང་རྒྱ་ཆེ་བའི་ཚོས་ཐམས་
ཅད་ཀྱི་དོན་དང་མཚན་ཐམས་ཅད་འདིར་འདུས་པར་སྟོན་ཅིང་
རྒྱུ་མཚན་དེས་གཅིག་ཤེས་ཀུན་གྲོལ་དུ་བསྒྲུབ་པར་མཛད་པའང་
ཡིན་ཏེ། འདི་ལ་དགོངས་ནས་བདེ་གཤེགས་ཕག་མོ་གྲུ་པས། རྣལ་
རྟོག་དང་ནི་ཉོན་མོངས་པ། །ཐམས་ཅད་འདུལ་བས་འདུལ་བ་ཡིན།
།རྣལ་པར་རྟོག་པ་ཆོས་སྐུ་རུ། །ངེས་པའི་ཤེས་པ་སྐྱེད་པའི་ས། །སྤྲོ
འདོགས་གཅད་ནས་གཅོད་པས་ན། །འདི་ནི་བླ་མའི་གདམས་ངག
ཡིན། །འཁོར་དང་མྱུང་ངན་འདས་པའི་ཚོས། །སེམས་སུ་རྟོགས་པས་
རྟོགས་ཆེན་ཡིན། །བཟང་རྟོག་ངན་རྟོག་ཐམས་ཅད་ཀུན། །ཡིད་ལ་

iii) The yoga of unity: the synonyms

19. *Free of mental engagement; this is mahāmudrā.*
Free of extremes; this is mahāmadhyamaka.
All-inclusive, it is also called mahāsandhi.
May I gain confidence that knowing one is realizing all.

Once you have realized innate timeless awareness just as it is, the unified yoga of resting in that equipoise is **free of all mental engagement. This is** called **mahāmudrā** ("great seal"). Other synonyms are enumerated. Because it is **free of all extremes** of embellishment, the **mahāmadhyamaka** ("great middle way") **is** also **this** very thing. In this is **included** the realization of **all** phenomena, so **it is also called mahāsandhi** ("great completion"). Through **knowing this one** thing, we aspire to **gain** the **confidence** of **realizing all** the secret vital points of the meaning of **all** phenomena.

The word "also" indicates that all characteristics and meanings of the vast and profound Dharma are included in this. Therefore this also establishes that "knowing one liberates all." Having pondered this, Sugata Pakmo Drupa stated:

All concepts and afflictions are tamed,
so this is the Vinaya.
It is the source of the certain knowledge
that all conceptual thoughts are dharmakāya.
As all embellishment is severed from within,
this is the instruction of the guru.
[Eternalism, nihilism, impositions, denials;
free of all such extremes, it is the middle way.
Being unutterable, unthinkable, and inexpressible,

མི་བྱེད་ཕྱུག་རྒྱུ་ཆེ། །ཕྱུག་བསྒྲལ་ནི་བས་ནི་བྱེད་ཡིན། །ཁྲིན་མོང་ས་
དང་ནི་རྣམ་རྟོག་ཀུན། །ལམ་དུ་སྐྱོང་བས་གསང་སྔགས་ཡིན། ། སེམས་དང་རྣམ་རྟོག་ཆོས་སྐུ་གསུམ། །དང་པོ་ལྷུན་ཅིག་སྐྱེས་པ་སྟེ།
།གདམས་པས་གཅིག་ཏུ་སྒྱུར་བའི་ཕྱིར། །ལྷན་ཅིག་སྐྱེས་སྦྱོར་ཞེས་
སུ་བཤད། །འདི་དང་བདུད་ལ་སོགས་པ་ཡི། །བར་གཅོད་ལ་ཡང་
བསྒྲགས་སོ་གསུངས། །ཞེས་དང་། ཨ་ནུ་གས་བུམ་སྐྱུབ་ཞལ་གདམས་
ལས་གསུངས་པ་ལྟ་བུས་མཚོན་ནོ། །

གཉིས་པ་ཉམས་རྟོགས་སྐྱེ་ཚུལ་ལ། ཉམས་དང་རྟོགས་པ་གཉིས་
ལས། དང་པོ། ཉམས་སྐྱེ་ཚུལ་ར་ནི།

ཞེན་པ་མེད་པའི་བདེ་ཆེན་རྒྱུན་ཆད་མེད། །མཚན་འཛིན་མེད་པའི་
འོད་གསལ་སྒྲིབ་གཡོག་བྲལ། །བློ་ལས་འདས་པའི་མི་རྟོག་ལྷུན་གྱིས་
གྲུབ། །ཚོལ་མེད་ཉམས་སྐྱོང་རྒྱུན་ཆད་མེད་པར་ཤོག

།ཅེས་གསུངས་ཏེ། དེ་ལྟར་ཞི་ལྷག་གི་རྩལ་འབྱོར་ལ་མཐའ་པར་
བཞག་པས་སྐྱོན་དང་བྲལ་བའི་ཉམས་གསུམ་སྐྱེ་སྟེ། ཞེན་པ་མེད་

it is the instruction on the Perfection of Wisdom.]
Since all phenomena of samsara and nirvana
are complete within mind, it is the great completion.
Not engaging good thoughts and bad thoughts
in the mind, it is the great seal.
It is pacification[39] since it pacifies suffering.
Since all afflictions and conceptual thoughts
are taken as the path, it is secret mantra.
Mind, thoughts, and dharmakāya—
these three are innate from the start.
Since they are applied as one by instructions,
they are taught as applied coemergence.
It is even acclaimed as the severance[40]
of obstructing demons, devils, and so on.[41]

This is also indicated by such teachings as the direct instructions for the vase consecration by Arāga.[42]

b) How experience and realization arise

i) How experience arises

20. *The great bliss free of attachment is continuous.*
Lucid clarity without fixation on attributes is free of obscuring
   veils.
Nonthought beyond intellect is spontaneously present.
May these experiences occur continuously without effort.

Three flawless experiences arise from resting in the equipoise of the yogas of calm abiding and higher insight: the experience of **continuous great bliss free of attachment**; the experience of

པའི་བདེ་བ་ཆེན་པོ་རྒྱུན་ཆད་མེད་པའི་ཉམས་དང་ཡུལ་ལ་མཚན་
མར་འཛིན་པ་མེད་པའི་རང་རིག་འོད་གསལ་སྒྱིབ་གཡོགས་བྲལ་
བའི་ཉམས་དང་། སྣའི་སྐྱོད་ཡུལ་ལས་འདས་པའི་མི་རྟོག་པ་སྤྲོང་པ་
ཉིད་ལྷུན་གྱིས་གྲུབ་པའི་ཉམས་ཏེ་བདེ་གསལ་མི་རྟོག་པའི་ཉམས་
གསུམ་གཞན་འབྱུང་དུ་རེ་བ་དང་མ་བྱུང་གིས་དོགས་པ་སོགས་
ཀྱིས་མི་བསྐྱོད་པར་གཤུག་མའི་ངང་དུ་ལ་བཟླས་ཀྱང་ཚུལ་མེད་
རང་ཤུགས་ཀྱིས་ཉམས་སྐྱོང་རྒྱུན་ཆད་མེད་པ་འབྱུང་བར་ཤོག་ཅིག་
ཅེས་པའོ། །དེ་ལས་ལྟོག་པ་ནི་སྐྱོན་ཅན་གོལ་ས་ཡིན་པས་རེ་དོགས་
འཛིན་ཞེན་མེད་པར་གཤུག་པའི་ངང་དུ་རོ་མཉམ་པས་བྱུང་འཇུག་
གི་ཆལ་རྟོགས་ཏེ་དེས་ཡོན་ཏན་ཐམས་ཅད་འབྱུང་སྟེ། དཔལ་ས་
ར་ཏན། སེམས་འགགས་པ་དང་རྐྱུང་འགགས་པ། །དཔལ་ལྡན་བླ་
མའི་མན་ངག་ཡིན། །ཞིས་གསུངས་པ་ལྟར་སེམས་ཟིན་པས་རྐྱུང་
ཟིན། དེས་དོས་སྐྱེ། དེས་བདེ་བ་སྐྱེ། དེ་ལ་བརྟེན་ནས་གསལ་བ་དང་
མི་རྟོག་པའང་འབྱུང་བས་གཏན་འདིས་ཁྲིད་སྒོལ་འདི་ལ་ཐབས་
ལམ་སོགས་ཆེད་དུ་མ་བསྐོམས་ཀྱང་ཪྟགས་བཅུ་ལ་སོགས་པ་སྐྲགས་
ལམ་གྱི་དོད་ཪྟགས་རྣམས་ཏེ་ལྷ་བ་བཞིན་འབྱུང་བ་སོགས་རྒྱ་ཆེར་
གསུངས་པ་ཡོད་དོ། །

གཉིས་པ་རྟོགས་པ་སྐྱེ་ཚུལ་ནི།

བཟང་ཞེན་ཉམས་ཀྱི་འཛིན་པ་རང་སར་གྲོལ། །དག་རྟོག་འཕྲལ་པ་
རང་བཞིན་དབྱིངས་སུ་དག །ཐ་མལ་ཤེས་པ་སྐྱང་སྔང་བྲལ་ཐོབ་
མེད། །སྤྲོས་བྲལ་ཆོས་ཉིད་བདེན་པ་རྟོགས་པར་ཤོག

lucid clarity free of obscuring veils, which is reflexive awareness **without fixation on** the **attributes** of objects; and the experience of **nonthought beyond** the sphere of **intellect, spontaneously present** emptiness. Reaching resolution within the innate state free of contamination, such as hopes for their arising or fears that they won't arise, we aspire that **these** felt **experiences occur continuously** on their own strength **without effort**.

Since the opposites of those are flawed deviations, cultivate equal taste within the innate state without hopes and fears, fixation, and clinging. That is the consummate expression of unity through which all good qualities will arise. Glorious Saraha said,

> Stilling the mind and stilling the winds
> is the glorious guru's esoteric instruction.[43]

As that suggests, controlling the mind causes control of the vital winds. That produces heat, which produces bliss. Based on that, clarity and nonthought will also occur. Through this vital point, even if you do not intentionally meditate on the path of methods in this guidance system, the signs of warmth in the Mantra Vehicle, such as the ten signs,[44] will arise just as they should. This and other subjects are taught extensively.

ii) How realization arises

21. *Attachment fixated on good experience subsides on its own.*
Delusion of bad thought is naturally pure in basic space.
Ordinary mind is free of acceptance and rejection, loss and
*   gain.*
May I realize the truth of unembellished true reality.

།ཅེས་གསུངས་ཏེ། བཤད་མ་ཐག་པའི་ཉམས་ལ་བཟང་རྟོིས་ཞེན་
འཛིན་སོགས་ཉམས་ཀྱི་འཛིན་པ་མཐའ་དག་རང་སར་གྲོལ་ཞིང༌།
རྣམ་གཡེང་གི་རྗེས་སུ་འབྲེང་བའི་ངན་རྟོག་འཁྱུལ་པ་ཐམས་ཅད་
ཀྱང་ཆེད་དུ་མ་སྤངས་ཀྱང་མཉམ་བཞག་གི་མཐུས་རང་བཞིན་གྱིས་
དེ་ཁོ་ན་ཉིད་ཀྱི་དབྱིངས་སུ་དག་པས་ཐ་མལ་གྱི་ཤེས་པ་ཞེས་གཏུག་
མའི་སེམས་དེ་ཉིད་མངོན་དུ་གྱུར་ཏེ། སྔང་བུ་སྐྱིབ་པའི་ཚོས་གང་
ཡང་སྣང་བ་མེད་པའི་ཚུལ་ཁོང་དུ་ཆུད་པ་དང༌། དེ་བཞིན་དུ་བླང་
བུ་གཉེན་པོའི་ཚོས་དང་སྤངས་པ་ལས་བྱུང་བའི་བྲལ་བ་དང་སྤངས་
བྲངས་བྱས་པས་ཐོབ་པའི་འབྲས་བུ་དང་བཅས་པ་དེ་དང་དེའི་
རང་བཞིན་དུ་མེད་ཅིང་མི་གནས་པའི་ཚུལ་རྗེ་ལྟ་བ་བཞིན་ཁོང་དུ་
ཆུད་པས་སྐྱེ་འགག་རྟག་ཆད་འགྲོ་འོང་གཅིག་ཐ་དད་སོགས་སྤྲོས་
པའི་མཐའ་ཐམས་ཅད་དང་བྲལ་བའི་ཚོས་ཉིད་ཀྱི་བདེན་པ་རྟོགས་
པར་ཧྲོག་ཅིག་ཅེས་པའོ། །འཁོར་འདས་བདེན་གཉིས་སོགས་གང་
ཡང་མི་དམིགས་པའི་གཉིས་མེད་ནི་ཚོས་ཉིད་ཀྱི་བདེན་པ་ཡིན་ལ་
དེ་རྟོགས་ན་བླང་དོར་སོགས་ཀྱི་མཚན་མ་སྒྲོག་རང་བཅལ་དུ་འགྲོ་
ཞིང་དེ་མིན་བླང་དོར་གྱི་མཚན་མ་རང་ཞིར་འགྱུར་མི་སྲིད་པ་ཀུན་
མཁྱེན་རྗེས་གསུངས་སོ། །

གསུམ་པ་བརྩེ་སྟོང་ཟུང་འཇུག་གི་ཉམས་ཞེན་ལ་སྐྱོན་པ་ལ་གཉིས།
སྐྱིང་རྗེ་རོས་བརྫང་བ། དེ་སྟོང་ཉིད་དང་ཟུང་དུ་འཇུག་ཚལ་ལོ།
།དང་པོ། སྐྱིང་རྗེ་རོས་བརྫང་བ་ནི།

Regarding those experiences just described, all **fixation on experience**, such as that it is **good**, or conceit, **attachment**, fixation and so on, **subside in their own** place. All the **delusional bad thoughts** that follow after total distraction [from meditation], even without being deliberately rejected, will be **naturally pure** in the **basic space** of suchness on the strength of your meditative equipoise. So-called **ordinary mind**, the innate mind itself, fully manifests. You should master the way of nonrejection of obscuring phenomena that are [normally] objects of **rejection**. Similarly, with what [is normally] **accepted**—the remedial teachings of antidotes, the **loss** produced by rejection, and the resulting **gain**s from rejection and acceptance—master precisely how that and its intrinsic nature are nonexistent and nonabiding. We aspire to **realize the truth** of **reality**, which is **free of** all extremes of **embellishment**, such as birth, cessation, permanence, extinction, going, coming, single, or many.

Nonduality is without any reference points, such as samsara and nirvana, the two truths, and so forth. This is the truth of reality. When that is realized, the ties to attributes, such as what to adopt and discard, are released. Barring that, it is not possible for the characteristics of adopting and discarding to resolve themselves, according to the omniscient lord.

c) The unity of love and emptiness

The aspiration to practice the unity of love and emptiness has two parts: identifying compassion and how that is unified with emptiness.

i) Identifying compassion

འགྲོ་བའི་རང་བཞིན་རྟག་ཏུ་སངས་རྒྱས་ཀྱང་། །མ་རྟོགས་དབང་
གིས་མཐའན་མེད་འཁོར་བར་འཁྱམས། །སྒྱུག་བསྒྲལ་མུ་མཐའན་མེད་
པའི་སེམས་ཅན་ལ། །བཟོད་མེད་སྙིང་རྗེ་རྒྱུད་ལ་སྐྱེ་བར་ཤོག །

།ཅེས་གསུངས་ཏེ། འགྲོ་བ་མ་ལུས་པའི་རང་བཞིན་ནི་དུས་རྟག་ཏུ་
སངས་རྒྱས་ཆོས་སྐུའི་ངོ་བོ་ཡིན་འདུག་ཀྱང་དེ་ལྟར་མ་རྟོགས་པའི་
དབང་གིས་མཐའན་མེད་པའི་འཁོར་བར་འཁྱམས། ཞིང་སྡུག་བསྔལ་
རྣམ་པ་སྣ་ཚོགས་མུ་མཐའན་མེད་པར་མྱོང་བའི་ཕ་མར་གྱུར་པའི་
སེམས་ཅན་ཐམས་ཅད་ལ་བཟོད་བླགས་མེད་པའི་སྙིང་རྗེ་དྲག་པོ་
རྒྱུན་མི་འཆད་པ་རྒྱུད་ལ་སྐྱེ་བར་ཤོག་ཅིག་ཅེས་པའོ། །བླ་མ་དགས་
པའི་མན་ངག་ཆུལ་བཞིན་ཉམས་སུ་བླངས་པས་གནས་ལུགས་
ཀྱི་དོན་གཞན་མ་རྟོགས་ཚེ་དེ་ལྟར་སྐྱེ་བའང་ཚོས་ཉིད་ཡིན་པར་
གསུངས་ཏེ། མདོ་ལས། བྱང་ཆུབ་སེམས་དཔའ་མཉམ་བཞག་པས།
།གོམས་པའི་སྟོབས་ཀྱིས་རྟོགས་པ་ན། །དངོས་འཛིན་གདོན་གྱིས་
ཟིན་པ་ལ། །ཁྱད་པར་དུ་ཡང་སྙིང་རྗེ་སྐྱེ། །ཞེས་དང་།

འཕགས་པ་ཀླུ་སྒྲུབ་ཀྱིས། དེ་ལྟར་སྟོང་པ་ཉིད་འདི་ནི། །རྣལ་འབྱོར་
པ་ཡིས་བསྒོམས་བྱས་ན། །གཞན་གྱི་དོན་ལ་ཆགས་པའི་བློ། །འབྱུང་
བར་འགྱུར་བ་ཐེ་ཚོམ་མེད། །ཅེས་དང་། མཉམ་མེད་དྭགས་པོས།

22. *Though the nature of migrators is ever buddha,*
they fail to realize it and wander endlessly in samsara.
May unbearable compassion be born in my being
for endlessly suffering sentient beings.

The nature of all **migrators** without exception has for**ever** been that of a **buddha,** present as the essence of dharmakāya. **Though** this is so, **they fail to realize it** as such and **wander endlessly in samsara,** experiencing an **endless** variety of **suffering.** We aspire that intense, unrelenting **compassion** that is **not possible to bear is born in our being for** all those **sentient beings** that have been our mothers and fathers.

At such time as the true meaning of the abiding nature arises through properly taking into practice the esoteric instructions of the holy guru, that is taught to be the true reality. It states in a sutra:

> The bodhisattva who has mastered equipoise
> on the strength of familiarization
> develops compassion particularly for those
> in the grip of the spirit of belief in reality.[45]

And Noble Nāgārjuna said,

> When a yogin thus meditates
> on this emptiness,
> an attitude of caring for others' welfare
> will no doubt arise.[46]

Incomparable Dakpo said,

དོན་དམ་རྟོགས་ན་བྱམས་སྙིང་རྗེ་གཞན་དོན་དུ་འབྱུང་བ་རྒྱུ་འབྲས་
ཡིན། ཉོན་མོངས་ཤུགས་ཀྱིས་ལྤོག་པ་ཡིན། ངོ་བོ་རྟོགས་ཟེར་ཡང་མི་
དགེ་བ་ལ་འཇུག་བྱམས་སྙིང་རྗེ་བྱང་ཆུབ་ཀྱི་སེམས་ཆུང་བར་འདུག་
ན་ངོ་བོ་མ་སྐྱེས་པ་ཡིན། བླ་མ་རྗེ་བཙུན་གྱིས་གསུངས་པ་དེ་ཡིན་
གསུངས།

དེས་ན་སྟོང་ཉིད་རྟོགས་པས་བདག་ལ་གཅེས་འཛིན་བྲལ་ཞིང་དེ་
ལྟར་མ་རྟོགས་པའི་འགྲོ་ལ་སྙིང་རྗེའི་དབང་གིས་སྙིད་ལས་གྲོལ་
ཡང་སྙིད་པ་བཟུང་ནས་འཁོར་བ་ཇི་སྙིད་དུ་སྙིད་པར་གནས་ཀྱང་
དེའི་སྐྱོན་གྱིས་མ་གོས་པར་ཆུའི་པད྄་བཞིན་འགྲོ་དོན་མཛད་པ་ནི་
རྒྱལ་སྲས་འཕགས་པ་ཞེས་བྱ་སྟེ། སྐྱུ་ཞབས་ཀྱིས།

བསམ་གཏན་བདེ་བ་ཕོར་ནས་ཀུན། །མཉར་མེད་པར་ཡང་འཛུག་
པར་བྱེད། །འདི་ནི་ངོ་མཚར་འདི་བསྔགས་འོས། །ཞེས་སོགས་རྒྱ་ཆེར་
གསུངས་པ་ལྟར་རོ།།

གཉིས་པ་ ཏེ་སྟོང་ཉིད་དང་རྲུང་དུ་འཇུག་ཚུལ་ནི།

བརྟོད་མེད་སྙིང་རྗེའི་ རྩལ་ཡང་མ་འགགས་པའི། །བརྗེ་དུས་ངོ་བོ་
སྟོང་དོན་རྗེན་པར་ཤར། །རྲུང་འཇུག་གོལ་ས་བྲལ་བའི་ལམ་མཚོག་
འདི། །འཕྲལ་མེད་ཉིན་མཚན་ཀུན་དུ་བསྒོམ་པར་ཤོག

།ཅེས་གསུངས་ཏེ། དེ་ལྟར་བརྟོད་བྲགས་མེད་པའི་སྙིང་རྗེ་ཆེན་པོའི་

> When you realize the absolute, love and com-
> passion and altruism develop—this is cause
> and effect. The opposite is true for the power
> of afflictions. To say you realize the essence but
> engage in nonvirtue with little love, compas-
> sion, and awakening mind [means that realiza-
> tion of] the essence has in fact not arisen. So
> said my guru Jetsun [Milarepa].[47]

Therefore, the realization of emptiness is free of self-
cherishing. Through the power of compassion for those who
do not have that realization, though you could be liberated
from existence, you hold on to existence and remain for as
long as existence exists. But like a lotus in water, you are not
sullied by its flaws. Someone who enacts the welfare of migrators in this way is known as an Exalted Child of the Victor.
This is taught widely, such as this by Nāgārjuna:

> Abandoning the bliss of concentration,
> they would even enter Incessant Hell.
> This is amazing and worthy of praise.[48]

ii) How compassion is unified with emptiness

23. *Unimpeded energy of unbearable compassion is love,*
the meaning of its empty essence exposed.
This supreme path of unity that never deviates;
may I meditate on this day and night without interruption.

The energy of such great unbearable compassion also
arises unimpededly and within that state is love. At that

ཚུལ་དེ་ཡང་མ་འགགས་པར་འཆར་བཞིན་པའི་དང་བཅུ་དུས་དེ་
ཉིད་ན་གནས་ལུགས་གཉིས་མེད་ཡེ་ཤེས་རོ་བོ་སྟོང་པ་ཉིད་ཀྱི་དོན་
ཡང་མཚོན་ལུས་རྟེན་པར་ཤར་བས་སྟོང་ཉིད་སྙིང་རྗེ་རོ་མཉམ་དུ་
འདྲེས་པའི་བྱུང་འཇུག་ནི་སྲིད་ཞིའི་གོལ་ས་བྲལ་བའི་ལམ་མཆོག་
མི་གནས་པའི་བྱང་འདས་བླ་མེད་རྟོགས་བྱུང་འཐོབ་པའི་རྒྱུ་དངོས་
ཡིན་པས་འདི་ཉིད་རོ་རྗེ་འཆང་གི་གོ་འཕང་ནས་ཐོབ་ཀྱི་བར་དུ་
རྒྱུན་གྱིས་འབྲལ་བ་མེད་པར་ཉིན་མཚན་ཀུན་ཏུ་བསྒོམ་པར་ཤོག་
ཅིག་ཅེས་པའོ། །

གསུམ་པ་སྟོང་པས་མཐར་དབྱུང་བ་ནི། ཤུགས་ལས་བསྣུན་ཏེ། དེ་
ལྟར་སྟོམས་པས་ཐམས་སུ་ཞེན་པའི་ཆལ་བསྣན་པ་ཉིད་གོམས་པ་
སྐྱོང་དུ་འགྱུར་བའི་ཕྱིར་མོས་གུས་སྒོམ་གྱི་མགོ་བོ་ལ་སྙིང་ཕུར་
བཅུགས་ཏེ་གཞི་བཅས། ཞིན་ལོག་སྒོམ་གྱི་ཁང་པས་ཚེ་འདིའི་འདོད་
འདུན་འཛིག་རྗེན་ཚོས་བཅུད་ཀྱི་གདོས་ཐག་བཅད། ཡངས་མེད་
སྒོམ་གྱི་དངོས་གཞི་སྒྲུབ་ཆུགས་རེ་ལྟར་དུ་བཅུན་པས་སྒོམ་མེད་
ཀྱི་རྒྱལ་སར་སླེག་པ་ནི་སྒོས་མེད་བླུ་སུ་ཀུའི་སྒྱོད་པ་ཞེས་སྒྱོད་པ་
རྣམས་ཀྱི་ནང་ནས་མཆོག་ཏུ་གྱུར་པ་བགགན་བཅུད་ཀུན་ཐོབ་རྒྱ་མཚོ་
གཤིགས་པའི་བཤུལ་ལས་རྒྱད་དུ་བྱུང་བ་སྟེ། གོང་དུ་སྒོམ་དོན་ཀུན་
ལ་རྒྱལ་སྒྱོང་སྒྱོད་པའི་མཆོག་གསུངས་པ་ཉིད་དོ། །

ལྷ་པ་ལས་མཐར་ཕྱིན་པའི་འབྲས་བུ་ལ་སྟོན་པ་ནི།

བསྐོམས་སྟོབས་ལས་བྱུང་སྦྱུན་དང་མཚོན་ཤེས་དང་། །ཞིམས་ཅན་

very moment, the timeless awareness of the nondual abiding nature, **the meaning of essential emptiness**, also manifests and is **exposed**. The **unity** of emptiness and compassion blended as a single taste is the **supreme path that never deviates** into existence or peace. This is the actual cause for attaining nonabiding nirvana or unsurpassable perfect awakening. Therefore, until the time of attaining the state of Vajradhara, we aspire to **meditate on this** constantly, **day and night without interruption** by circumstances.

C) Reaching the ultimate through conduct

This is presented implicitly because one attains full mastery through familiarizing oneself with this very teaching on how to practice meditation in this manner. "Devotion, the head of meditation," means that an unwavering heart is the foundation. "Revulsion, the foot of meditation," is to decisively cut off the yearning desires of this life and the eight worldly concerns. "Nondestraction, the body of meditation," is to firmly establish practice like a mountain. Therefore, to reach the domain of nonmeditation, the so-called unembellished *bhusuku* conduct[49] is the most excellent of all the conducts. It is the path traveled by the ocean of Kagyü adepts, left as an amazing legacy. The energy training in all the meditation topics described above are themselves the supreme conduct. So it is said.

5. Aspiration for the ultimate result of the path

24. *With the eyes and clairvoyances produced by potent*
    meditation,

སྐྱེན་བྱས་སངས་རྒྱས་ཞིང་རབ་སྦྱངས། །སངས་རྒྱས་ཆོས་རྣམས་
འགྲུབ་པའི་སྨོན་ལམ་རྟོགས། །རྟོགས་སྐྱེན་སྤྱངས་གསུམ་མཐར་ཕྱིན་
སངས་རྒྱས་ཤོག །

།ཅེས་གསུངས་ཏེ། དེ་ལྟར་ཚོས་གྱུས་བླ་མའི་བྱིན་རླབས་ཀྱི་ཉེ་ལམ་
ལ་བརྟེན་པའི་ཕྱག་རྒྱ་ཆེན་པོའི་གདམས་ངག་ཕྱིན་ཅི་མ་ལོག་པ་
བསྒོམས་པའི་སྟོབས་ཀྱིས་བྱུང་བའི་འབྲས་བུ་སྐུན་ལུ་དང་། མཚོན་
པར་ཤེས་པ་དྲུག་རྣམས་ཡོངས་སུ་དག་པའི་ཡོན་ཏན་དང་ལྡན་
པས་སེམས་ཅན་ཐམས་ཅད་སྐྱེན་པར་བྱས་ཤིངད། སངས་རྒྱས་ཀྱི་
ཞིང་རབ་འབྱམས་མཐའ་ཡས་པ་སྦྱངས་ནས། སངས་རྒྱས་ཀྱི་ཆོས་
གཞན་དང་ཐུན་མོང་མ་ཡིན་པའི་སྐུ་དང་ཡེ་ཤེས་ཡོན་ཏན་ཕྲིན་
ལས་རྣམས་ཡོངས་སུ་གྲུབ་པའི་སྨོན་ལམ་འབྱམ་ཐུག་བཅུ་འབོར་
དང་བཅས་པ་མཐའ་དག་རྟོགས་པ་དང་། དེ་ལྟར་རྟོགས་སྐྱེན་སྦྱངས་
གསུམ་ཐམས་ཅད་མཐར་ཕྱིན་ནས་བླ་ན་མེད་པ་རྟོགས་པའི་སངས་
རྒྱས་ཀྱི་གོ་འཕང་མྱུར་དུ་ཐོབ་པར་ཤོག་ཅིག་ཅེས་པའོ། །དེའང་ལས་
དུས་སུ་ཐོག་མར་མཚོན་ཤེས་སོགས་བསྐྱེད་ནས་རིམ་གྱིས་རྟོགས་
སྐྱེན་སྤྱངས་གསུམ་མཐར་དབྱུང་དགོས་པས་ན་འདིར་ཡང་ཐོག་
མར་སྤྱན་དང་མཚོན་ཤེས་ཞིང་གསུངས་པ་སྟེ། དེ་ལ་སྤྱན་ལྟ་ནི།
མདོ་ལས། བྱང་ཆུབ་སེམས་དཔའི་ཤའི་མིག་གིས་དཔག་ཚད་བརྒྱ་
ནས་སྟོང་གསུམ་གྱི་སྟོང་ཆེན་པོའི་འཇིག་བརྟེན་གྱི་ཁམས་མཐོང་
བར་གསུངས་པ་ནི། ཤའི་སྤྱན་དང་། རྒྱལ་ཆེན་བཞི་རིས་པ་རྣམས་
ནས་འོག་མིན་བར་གྱི་ལྷ་རྣམས་ཀྱི་ལྷའི་མིག་དེ་ནི་བྱང་ཆུབ་སེམས་

sentient beings are matured and buddha fields refined.
Aspirations for accomplishing buddha qualities are fulfilled.
May I become buddha, the ultimate fulfillment, maturation,
    and refinement.

The five **eyes and** the six **clairvoyances** are the result **produced by** the **potent meditation** on unerring instructions of mahāmudrā based on the fast path of devotion and the blessings of the guru. **With** these completely pure qualities, all **sentient beings are matured and** the infinite **buddha realms** without limit are **refined**. A million **aspirations** and their offshoots **for accomplishing** other **buddha qualities** and extraordinary bodies, awarenesses, qualities, and activities are totally **fulfilled**. In this way, after reaching the **ultimate** stage of these three—**fulfillment, maturation, and refinement**—we aspire to quickly attain the state of unsurpassed perfect **buddha**.

At the time of the path, first the clairvoyances and so on are produced and then gradually the fulfillment, maturation, and refinement must be brought to consummation. Therefore, here the eyes and clairvoyances were taught first.

The five eyes [or sights] are taught in the sutras:

(1) With the physical eyes the bodhisattvas can see from one hundred leagues up to all the billion world realms in the universe. (2) The divine eye is possessed by all the gods from the realms of the four great kings up to the unsurpassed realm Akaniṣṭha. It is said that bodhisattvas fully comprehend that sight, but the gods do not comprehend the divine eye that bodhisattvas possess. That is because over and above that

དཔའ་རབ་ཏུ་ཤེས་ལ་བྱང་ཆུབ་སེམས་དཔའི་ས་ལྔའི་ཤིག་དེ་ནི་ལྷ་
དེ་རྣམས་ཀྱིས་མི་ཤེས་པར་གསུངས་པས་ལྔའི་ཤིག་དེ་ལས་བྱུང་
པར་འཐགས་པ་ཕྱོགས་བཅུའི་སེམས་ཅན་ཐམས་ཅད་ཀྱི་འཆི་འཕོ་
དང་སྐྱེ་བ་གཟིགས་པ་ལྔའི་ཤྱུན་དང་། བདག་མེད་དེ་བཞིན་རྟོགས་
པའི་ཤེས་རབ་ནི་ཤེས་རབ་ཀྱི་ཤྱུན་དང་། སྤྲ་དཔོན་དཔྱིག་གཉིན་
ཀྱིས་བཞིད་པ་ལྟར་གནས་དང་གནས་མིན་མཁྱེན་པའི་སྟོབས་མ་
གཏོགས་སྟོབས་དགུ་པོ་རྣམས་ནི་ཆོས་ཀྱི་ཤྱུན་དང་། ཆོས་ཐམས་ཅད་
རྣམ་པ་ཐམས་ཅད་དུ་མངོན་པར་རྟོགས་པ་རྟོགས་པ་ནི་སངས་
རྒྱས་ཀྱི་ཤྱུན་ཏེ་ལྔའོ། །མངོན་ཤེས་དྲུག་ནི། རྫུ་འཕྲུལ་ཀྱི་ཚེ་འཕུལ་
མཐའ་ཡས་པར་སྟོན་པའི་རྫུ་འཕྲུལ་མངོན་པར་ཤེས་པ། མཐའ་ཡས་
པའི་ཞིང་གི་སྐྲ་བོས་པའི་ལྔའི་རྣ་བ་མངོན་པར་ཤེས་པ་སེམས་ཅན་
ཐམས་ཅད་ཀྱི་སེམས་ཀྱི་ཚུལ་ཇི་ལྟ་བར་སོ་སོར་ཤེས་པའི་གཞན་
སེམས་མངོན་པར་ཤེས་པ། སེམས་ཅན་རྣམས་ཀྱི་སྐྱེ་འཆི་ལས་དང་
འབྲས་བུའི་ཚུལ་དང་བཅས་ཤེས་པའི་ལྔའི་མིག་མངོན་པར་ཤེས་པ།
སྐྱིབ་ཐོགས་མཐའ་དག་ངོ་བོ་ཉིད་ཀྱི་མི་གནས་པས་རབ་ཏུ་སྦྱངས་
པའི་ཟག་པ་ཟད་པ་མངོན་པར་ཤེས་པ་དང་དྲུག་གོ །ལྔའི་མིག་ལྔ་
མ་རྣམ་སྨིན་ལས་སྐྱེས་པ་དང་། ཕྱི་མ་བསྐོམས་སྟོབས་ལས་སྐྱེས་པའི་
ཁྱད་པར་དང་། སྒྱུར་ཤྱུན་དང་མངོན་ཤེས་རྣམས་ལས་དུས་ནས་རིམ་
པར་ཇེ་གསལ་ལ་སོང་བས་སངས་རྒྱས་ཀྱི་བར་ཡོངས་སུ་རྟོགས་པས་
ཤེན་ཏུ་རྣམ་པར་དག་ཅིང་མཐར་ཐུག་པ་སྟེ་ཡུལ་མ་ལུས་པ་ལ་རྒྱ་

divine eye, [bodhisattvas] can see the death, transition, and birth of every sentient being in the ten directions with their divine sight. (3) The wisdom eye is the wisdom that properly realizes nonself. (4) The dharma eye, according to Ācārya Vasubandhu, is comprised of nine out of ten strengths, excepting the strength of knowing what is appropriate and inappropriate. (5) The buddha eye is the realization of the complete perfection of all aspects of phenomena. These are the five eyes.

The six clairvoyances:

(1) The clairvoyance of miracles is the display of infinite miraculous apparitions. (2) The clairvoyance of divine ears is the ability to hear the sounds of infinite realms. (3) The clairvoyance of others' minds is knowledge of exactly what is occurring in the modality of the individual minds of all sentient beings. (4) [The clairvoyance of past existences is knowledge of the continuum of past and future lives of all individual sentient beings].[50] (5) The clairvoyance of the divine eye is the knowledge of the ways of birth and death, as well as the karmic causes and results, of all sentient beings. (6) The clairvoyance of the cessation of dissipation is their complete elimination through [knowing that] infinite obscurations are not present in essence.

The difference in the two divine eyes is that the former arises from karmic ripening, while the latter arises on the strength of meditation. In general, the eyes and clairvoyances are gradually clarified at the time of the path. Through that process, they are completely perfected on the level of a buddha. Then they are utterly pure and ultimate, such that one enters without limitation or bias or restrictions [into the knowledge of]

ཆད་ཕྱོགས་རིས་ཆགས་ཐོགས་མེད་པར་འཇུག་པ་སོགས་ཕུན་ཚོང་
མིན་པ་ཉིད་དོ། །

སེམས་ཅན་སྐྱིན་པ་ནི། ཟས་སྐྱིན་ནས་བཟར་རུང་བ་ལྟར་གདུལ་བྱ་
རྣམས་སྨྲང་དུ་སྦྱོང་རུང་དང་གཉེན་པོ་སྐྱེ་རུང་དུ་སྐྱིན་པ་སྟེ། དབྱེ་
ན། བྲལ་བར་སྐྱིན་པ་སོགས་བཅུད་མདོ་རྒྱུན་ལས་གསུངས་སོ། །ཞིང་
སྦྱངས་པ་ནི། བཟང་སྤྱོད་ལས། གང་ཡང་དུས་གསུམ་དག་གི་ཞིང་
བཀོད་པ། །དེ་དག་རྒྱལ་གཅིག་སྟེང་དུ་མཛེན་པར་སྒྲུབ། །ཅེས་དང་།
ཞིང་རྣམས་རྒྱ་མཚོ་རྣམ་པར་དག་བྱེད་ཅིང་། །ཞེས་པ་ལྟར་ཞིང་
མཐའ་ཡས་སྒྲུབ་པ་དང་དེ་དག་བདེ་བ་ཅན་ལྟར་ཡོངས་སུ་དག་
པར་སྟོང་བའོ། །སངས་རྒྱས་ཀྱི་ཆོས་ནི། སངས་རྒྱས་ཉིད་ཨ་གཏོགས་
བྱང་སེམས་འཕགས་པས་ཀྱང་ཕྱོགས་ཚམ་ལས་མཚོན་མི་ནུས་པར་
གསུངས་པས་བྱིས་པའི་བློའི་སྤྱོད་ཡུལ་ལས་འདས་མོད་ཀྱང་ཕྱོགས་
སུ་བསྟུས་པ་ན་གོང་ལྟར་སྐུ་དང་ཡེ་ཤེས་

all phenomena without exception, and so forth. Thus this is not in common [with those qualities at the time of the path].

Maturing sentient beings:

Just as food must be ripe to be edible, those to be trained are matured so that they are ready to eliminate what is to be eliminated and ready to develop the antidotes. There are eight divisions explicated in the *Adornment of the Sūtras*[51] and elsewhere, such as the maturing in freedom [from afflictions]. As for refining the realms, it says in the *Prayer of Samantabhadra's Conduct*:

> Whatever array of pure realms there are in the three times,
> they are all manifested upon a single atom.

And:

> [May I] totally purify an ocean of realms.[52]

Thus infinite realms are established and refined into total purity, like the Realm of Bliss (Sukhāvatī).

Buddha qualities:

It is said that other than a buddha, even the exalted bodhisattvas cannot demonstrate more than a fraction [of those qualities], so it is certainly beyond the intellectual sphere of childish people. Nevertheless, if one were to pose an approximate summary, it is said that they are subsumed into the

ཡོན་ཏན་ཕྲིན་ལས་རྣམས་ཀྱིས་ཉེ་བར་བསྐུས་པར་གསུངས་པས།
འདིར་ཡི་གེ་མང་ཕྱིར་མ་སྤྲོས་ཀྱང་བྱམས་ཆོས་ཆེ་བ་གསུམ་སོགས།
ལས་ཤེས་པར་བྱ་ཞིང་མདོ་ཚམ་བདེ་སྟོན་ཤེས་བྱའི་འགྱེལ་བར་ཡང་
གསལ་ལོ། །ཞེར་བྱུང་ལས་ཀྱི་རིམ་པ་ཅུང་ཟད་སྟོན་ན། གྲུབ་ཆེན་
ནུ་རོས་པས་ཕྱུག་རྒྱ་ཆེན་པོ་ཆིག་བསྐུས་སུ་གསུངས་པ་ལྟར་བརྒྱུད་
པ་འདིའི་ཐུན་མོང་མ་ཡིན་པའི་ཆོས་སྐད་དུ་མཚད་པ་རྐ་འབྱོར་
བཞི་རིས་ནི། ཞི་གནས་ཀྱི་སེམས་རྩེ་གཅིག་པ་ཐོབ་ནས་གནས་པ་
ལ་ལྷག་མཐོང་ཕར་ཞིང་བདེ་གསལ་མི་རྟོག་པའི་ཉམས་འཁོར་ཡུག་
ཏུ་འབྱུང་བ་རྩེ་གཅིག་གི་རྣལ་འབྱོར་དང་། སྣང་སེམས་ཀྱིས་བསྐུས་
པའི་ཆོས་མཐའ་དག་ཆོས་དབྱིངས་བདེ་བ་ཆེན་པོའི་རང་བཞིན་
ལས་མ་འདས་པར་མཐོང་བས་གཉིས་ཆོས་ཀྱི་སྤྲོས་འཇིན་ཐབས་
ཅད་རང་གྲོལ་དུ་སོང་ཞིང་སྤྲོང་ཉིད་སྙིང་རྗེ་ཟུང་འཇུག་གི་ཡེ་ཤེས་
ལྷག་མཐོང་མཆན་ཉིད་པ་ཐོབ་པས་ཞི་ལྷག་གི་རྣལ་འབྱོར་རྗེ་ལྟ་
བར་ཟུང་དུ་ཆུད་པ་སྤྲོས་བྲལ་གྱི་རྣལ་འབྱོར་དང་། དེ་གོང་ནས་གོང་
དུ་གོམས་པས་ཆོས་ཐམས་ཅད་དུ་མ་རོ་གཅིག་ཏུ་རྟོགས་ཤིང་ཆོལ་
མེད་ཀྱི་ཡེ་ཤེས་ནུས་པ་མེད་པར་སྣང་སེམས་དངོས་སུ་འདྲེས་པ་རོ་
གཅིག་གི་རྣལ་འབྱོར་དང་། བསྐོམས་པའི་འོད་གསལ་དང་གཞིའི་
འོད་གསལ་གཅིག་ཏུ་འདྲེས་པས་གནས་ལུགས་ཀྱི་སྐྱབ་གཡོག་

kāyas, awarenesses, qualities, and enlightened activities that have been taught before. These will not be elaborated upon here for fear of too many words, but should be learned from the three great Maitreya Dharmas.[53] It is also clarified more succinctly in the commentary on the aspects to know in the *Aspiration Prayer for the Realm of Bliss.*[54]

Supplement: a brief description of the stages of the path

As the great adept Nāropa taught in *Concise Words on Mahāmudrā*,[55] this lineage employs an uncommon Dharma terminology, that of the four yogas.

(1) The yoga of single-pointed attention (*rtse gcig*): once the single-pointed focus of calm abiding is attained, higher insight arises within that state of abiding and the experiences of bliss, clarity, and nonthought arise all the time.

(2) The yoga free of elaboration (*spros bral*): by seeing that the whole range of phenomena that are appearing in the mind do not transcend the nature of the great bliss of the realm of phenomena, you are naturally liberated from all fixation on the dualistic elaborations regarding phenomena. You attain authentic higher insight, the unity of emptiness and compassion, and enter into the yoga where calm abiding and higher insight are properly unified.

(3) The yoga of one taste (*ro gcig*): As you become ever more familiarized with that, you realize that the multitude of all phenomena have but one taste. Appearance and mind are truly blended in the effortless gnosis that never declines.

(4) The yoga of nonmeditation (*sgom med*): The lucid clarity of meditation and the lucid clarity of the basic ground blend into one, by which all the obscurations that cover the

མཐའ་དག་གཞི་མེད་དུ་དངས། མཐུག་རྟེས་ཀྱི་མཚམས་ཞིག་མཐར་
ཐུག་གི་ཡོན་ཏན་ཐམས་ཅད་སྒྱུན་གྱུབ་ཏུ་འབྱུང་བ་སྐོམ་མེད་ཀྱི་
རྣལ་འབྱོར་ཞེས་བུ་སྟེ། དེ་བཞི་ལ་སོ་སོའི་མཚན་ཉིད་རྣལ་མ་རྟོགས་
པ་དང། ཐལ་ཆེར་རྟོགས་པ་དང། ཡོངས་སུ་རྟོགས་པའི་རིམ་པས་
རྒྱུང་འབྱིང་ཆེན་པོར་དབྱེ་བས་བཅུ་གཉིས་སུ་འགྱུར་ལ་དེ་དག་ཐར་
ཐྱིན་ཐེག་པའི་ལམ་དང་སྦྱར་ན། རྩེ་གཅིག་གསུམ་ཚོགས་ལམ། སྤོས་
བྲལ་རྒྱུང་འབྲིང་སྦྱོར་ལམ། ཆེན་པོ་མཐོང་ལམ། རོ་གཅིག་གསུམ་
དང་སྐོམ་མེད་རྒྱུང་འབྲིང་སྒོམ་ལམ། སྒོམ་མེད་ཆེན་པོ་མཐར་ཐྱིན་
པའི་ལམ་དུ་གསུངས་པ་དང། ཡང་རྒྱུང་ཀྱི་དགོངས་པ་སེམས་འགྲེལ་
སྦོར་དྲུག་རྣམས་ལས་གསུངས་པ་ལྟར་སྦོར་ལམ་ངེས་འབྱེད་ཏིང་ངེ་
འཛིན་ཀྱིས་ས་བཅུ་གཉིས་དང་སྦྱར་ནས་སྒོམ་མེད་ཆེན་པོ་མཐོང་
ལམ་དུ་བཞེད་པ་གཉིས་གདུལ་བྱའི་བློ་རིས་ལ་སྤྱས་ཏེ་དགོངས་གཞི་
དགོས་དབང་གིས་གསུངས་པའི་ཐྱིར། ངེས་པའི་དོན་གང་དུ་གནས་
ནི་མཁས་གྲུབ་ཚོས་སྒྲུབ་ཤྱན་པའི་ཞལ་གྱི་བདུད་རྩི་དངོས་སུ་མྱོང་
བ་དང། རྒྱལ་འབྱོར་རང་ཉིད་རྟོགས་གོམས་རབ་ཏུ་གྱུར་ཚེ་བསྒོམས་
བྱུང་ཤེས་རབ་ཀྱིས་ངེས་པར་འགྱུར་བའོ། །

ཀླུ་བའི་ས་བཅད་གསུམ་པ་སྨོན་ལམ་ཀྱི་མཐུག་བསྟུ་བ་ལ་གཉིས།
དངོས་དང། མཇད་བྱང་ངོ་། །དང་པོ་ ཌངོས་༢ ནི།

abiding nature become transparent in their lack of a basis. The boundary between resting in equipoise and subsequent attainment vanishes. All the qualities of the ultimate state are spontaneously present.

Those four each have three levels: their attributes being underdeveloped, mostly developed, and fully developed—thus dividing into small, middle, and great—twelve stages in all. Compared with the paths of the Perfections Vehicle, it is taught that the three levels of single-pointed yoga correspond to the path of accumulation. The lesser and middle levels of freedom from elaboration correspond to the path of application, and the greater to the path of seeing. The three levels of one taste and the lesser level of nonmeditation are the path of meditation, and the greater level of nonmeditation corresponds to the ultimate path. Or, according to the intent of the tantras, *Bodhisattva Commentaries*,[56] and the six-branch yoga,[57] the absorption of definite discrimination on the path of application is associated with the twelve stages (*sa*; Skt. *bhūmi*), and the greater level of nonmeditation to the path of seeing. These two viewpoints depend upon the mental capacity of those to be trained, because they are taught out of the necessity to have a basis in Buddha's thought. As to where the definitive meaning lies, it will become certain by means of the wisdom from actually tasting the nectar from the mouths of those learned adepts with the eye of Dharma and from the result of meditation when the yogin truly attains excellent realization and familiarization.

III. Concluding summary of the aspiration
This has two parts: the main part and the colophon.

ཕྱོགས་བཅུའི་རྒྱལ་བ་སྲས་བཅས་ཐུགས་རྗེ་དང་། །རྫུ་དགར་དགེ་བ་རྗེ་སྐྱེད་ཡོད་པའི་མཐུས། །དེ་ལྟར་བདག་དང་སེམས་ཅན་ཐམས་ཅད་ཀྱི། །སྨོན་ལམ་རྣམ་དག་རྗེ་བཞིན་འགྲུབ་གྱུར་ཅིག

།ཅེས་གསུངས་ཏེ། ཕྱོགས་བཅུར་བཞུགས་པའི་རྒྱལ་བ་སྲས་དང་བཅས་པ་རྣམས་ཀྱི་དམིགས་པ་མེད་པའི་ཐུགས་རྗེ་ཆེན་པོ་དང་། རྣམ་པར་དཀར་བའི་དགེ་བ་བགྱིས་པ་དང་གཞན་གྱི་དགེ་བ་ལ་ཡི་རང་བགྱིས་པ་རྗེ་སྐྱེད་ཡོད་པའི་མཐུ་ལ་བརྟེན་ནས་དེ་ལྟར་འདིར་བསྔན་གྱི་སྨོན་ལམ་ཉིད་གཙོར་བྱས་ནས་བདག་དང་སེམས་ཅན་ཐམས་ཅད་ཀྱི་སྨོན་ལམ་རྣམ་པར་དག་པ་རྗེ་སྐྱེད་ཅིག་བཏབ་པ་དེ་ཐམས་ཅད་དེ་བཞིན་དུ་འགྲུབ་པར་གྱུར་ཅིག་ཅེས་པའོ། །

གཉིས་པ། །མཛད་བྱང་ངི།

ཅེས་དོན་ཕྱག་རྒྱ་ཆེན་པོའི་སྨོན་ལམ་ཞེས་བྱ་བ་རྗེ་རང་བྱུང་རྡོ་རྗེས་མཛད་པའོ།

།ཞེས་སོ། །དེ་ལྟར་དུས་གསུམ་རྒྱལ་བ་ཀུན་གྱི་བགྲོད་པ་གཅིག་པའི་ལམ་མཆོག་མདོ་རྒྱུད་མན་ངག་ཐམས་ཅད་ཀྱི་བརྗོད་བྱ་མཐར་ཐུག་གྲུབ་པའི་སྟི་མེས་མདའ་བསྟན་ཡང་སྲས་ཀྱི་གདམས་ངག་ཕྱོགས་པའི་སངས་རྒྱས་ཀྱི་བསྟ་མེད་རྡོ་རྗེའི་ལྱང་གིས་གསལ་བར་བསྟན་པ་བཞིན་དུ་མཉམ་མེད་ཆོས་ཀྱི་རྒྱལ་པོ་དགགས་པོ་ལྷ་རྗེས་རྒྱ་ཆེར

A. Main part

25. By the compassion of the ten-direction victors and their
*   heirs,*
and the power of whatever pure virtue there is,
may my pure aspirations and those of all beings
all be fulfilled just as intended.

Based on **the** nonreferential great **compassion** of the **victors and their heirs** who dwell in **the ten directions**, and through **the power of whatever** totally **pure virtue** has been done and the rejoicing in whatever virtue **there is** that has been done by others, just like that, may whatever totally **pure aspirations** have been made by **me and all sentient beings**, headed mainly by this aspiration prayer that has been presented here, **all be fulfilled just as intended.**

B. Colophon

The Aspiration Prayer of Definitive Mahāmudrā *is by Lord Rangjung Dorjé.*

This is the single supreme path traveled by all the victors of the three times; the ultimate subject matter of all sutras, tantras, and esoteric instructions; and the instructions of the father–child lineage of the great ancestral adept, the Archer (Saraha). This doctrine, illuminated by the undeceiving vajra scriptures of the perfect Buddha, was exhaustively clarified by the unequaled king of Dharma, Dakpo Lhajé (Gampopa), and so it is the spiritual practice of the king of Kagyü adepts. This aspiration teaches clearly in a few summarized words the meaning of the ground,

གསལ་བར་མཛད་པས་བཀའ་བརྒྱུད་གྲུབ་ཐོབ་རྒྱལ་པོའི་ཐུགས་

དམ་ཊེས་དོན་ཕྱག་རྒྱ་ཆེན་པོར་གྲགས་པའི་གཞི་ལམ་འབྲས་གསུམ་

གྱི་དོན་རྣམས་ཚིག་ཉུང་འདུས་ཀྱིས་གསལ་བར་སྟོན་པའི་སྟོན་ལས་

འདི་ཉིད། བདག་ཅག་གི་འདྲེན་པ་དྲུག་པ་སེངྒེའི་རྣམ་པར་རོལ་པ་

ཐམས་ཅད་མཁྱེན་པ་དཔལ་ལྡན་གཀྲ་པ་རང་བྱུང་རྡོ་རྗེའི་ཞལ་སྔ་

ནས་ཀྱིས་རྗེས་འཇུག་རྣམས་ལ་ཐུགས་བརྩེ་བས་གདམས་པའི་ཕྱིར་

ནན་ཏན་དུ་འབད་པར་གཅེས་ཏེ། ཀུན་མཁྱེན་མི་བསྐྱོད་རྡོ་རྗེའི་

ཞལ་ནས། ཆོས་ཆྱལ་འདི་ལ་བཀའ་བརྒྱུད་འདི་པ་ཐུགས་ཚིམ་པོ་

ཆེར་བཟུང་ནས་དམ་ཆོས་བླ་ན་མེད་པར་མཛད་པས། སྐལ་ལྡན་གྱི་

སྐྱེ་བུ་དག་རབ་ཏོགས་པ། འབྲིང་ཉམས། མཐའ་མ་འང་གོ་བའི་ཤེས་

རབ་ཚམ་གྱིས་ཀྱང་ཉམས་སུ་ཅི་ཡོང་ལ་འབད་པར་གྱིས། ཤིག་ཅེས་

འདོམས་པར་མཛད་དོ། ཌེས་དོན་ཞབ་མོའི་ཚལ་ལ་དང་འདོད་

ཡིད་ཆེས་ཀྱི་དད་པས་འཇུག་པ་ལྷ་ཅི་སྟོན། ཐོས་ནས་ཡིད་མ་ཆེས་

པར་ཐེ་ཚོམ་དུ་གྱུར་པ་རྣམས་ཀྱང་ཐེ་ཚོམ་གྱི་ཉེས་པས་རེ་ཞིག་ངན་

གྲོར་སོང་ཡང་། ཐབ་དོན་ཐོས་པའི་བྱིན་མཐུས་ཡུན་མི་རིང་བར་དེ་

ལས་ཐར་ནས་བྱང་ཆུབ་འཐོབ་པར་སངས་རྒྱས་ཀྱིས་ལུང་བསྟན་

བསྟལ་བའི་ལོ་རྒྱུས་དུ་མ་མདོ་སྟེ་རྣམས་ལས་འབྱུང་ཞིང་སྩོབ་

དཔོན་སྐྱ་ཞབས་ཀྱིས་ཀྱང་། བསོད་ནམས་རྒྱུང་བས་ཆོས་འདི་ལ། །ཐེ་

ཚོམ་ཙམ་ཡང་མི་སྐྱེ་སྟེ། །འདི་ལ་ཐེ་ཚོམ་སྐྱེས་པས་ཀྱང་། །སྲིད་པ་

དུལ་པོར་བྱེད་པར་འགྱུར། །ཞེས་གསུངས་ཤིང་དད་པ་གསུམ་གྱིས་

འབད་པའི་ཐན་ཡོན་ནི། འདི་དང་མ་འབྲེལ་བའི་དགེ་བ་རྒྱ་ཆེན་

པོ་བསྐལ་པ་གང་གྷའི་ཀྱུང་གི་བྱེ་སྙེད་དུ་བསྒྲུབ་པའི་བསོད་ནམས་

path, and fruition of the renowned definitive mahāmudrā. Our guide, the [future] sixth lion emanation,[58] omniscient glorious Karmapa Rangjung Dorjé, spoke this instruction out of love for future followers. Therefore, cherish it and strive in persistent practice. The all-knowing Mikyö Dorjé counseled:

> In this Dharma system, this Kagyüpa, [when you] deeply appreciate its great value, you make it the unsurpassable holy Dharma. Then, the best of the fortunate disciples will have realization, the average will have experiences, and even the least of them will gain at least the wisdom of understanding. Whatever you take into practice, preserver in it.[59]

There is no need to discuss those who possess enthusiastic, longing, and confident faith in this profound system of the definitive meaning. Even those flawed doubters who hear it but don't believe it will go to the lower realms for a while, but not for very long. The power of the blessings of hearing the profound meaning will liberate them from there and they will gain enlightenment. There are many such stories of prophesies by the Buddha in the sutras. Also, Master Nāgārjuna said,

> Those of little merit will not doubt this Dharma.
> But even if they do, it will still shred existence.[60]

Regarding the benefits of exerting yourself with the three kinds of faith, there is greater benefit in hearing the mere words and developing interest and confidence in this kind of Dharma that teaches the abiding nature of suchness than in

ལས་ཀྱང་། བསམ་གྱིས་མི་ཁྱབ་པ་དེ་ཕོ་ན་ཉིད་ཀྱི་གནས་ལུགས་སྟོན་
པའི་ཚོས་ཆུལ་འདི་ལྷ་བུའི་ཆིག་ཚམ་ཐོས་ནས་མོས་པ་དང་ལྷན་
པས་ཡིད་ཆེས་ན་ཐན་ཡོན་ཆེ་བར་བགའ་དང་བསྟུན་བཅོས་རྣམས་
ལས་རྒྱ་ཆེར་གསུངས་སོ། །མདོ་རྒྱུད་མན་ངག་ཐབ་དོན་ཀུན་དང་
མཐུན། །ཕྱིན་ཅི་ལོག་ནས་བཔབས་ཀྱིས་ཀུན་ལས་ཁྱད་པར་འཕགས། །དང་
བཙོན་ཧེར་གསུམ་ལྡན་པ་ལྷ་ཅི་སྐོས། །སྐྱོངས་ཅུལ་མོས་གུས་དག་
པོས་འབད་བྱས་ཀྱང་། །ཤྱིད་མཚོ་སྐྱིག་རྗེས་རྒྱ་ཚམ་བྱེད་པ་ནི། །རྡོ་རྗེ་
འཆང་ནས་རྩ་བའི་བླ་མའི་བར། །ཧོགས་པ་དོན་གྱི་བརྒྱུད་པ་མ་ཆད་
པས། །ཚ་བརྒྱུད་བླ་མའི་བྱིན་རྣབས་ཁོ་ནའི་མཐུ། །དེ་ཕྱིར་འདི་སྟྱོད་
སྐལ་པ་ལྡན་དུས་འདིར། །མི་དབང་རིན་ཆེན་བདུན་དང་དཔལ་
འབྱོར་ཀྱང་། །རྒྱ་མིང་འདུ་བར་གསུངས་ན་སྟྱིག་སྱུག་གཱི། །ཚོ་འདིའི་
བུ་བ་འཇིག་བརྟེན་ཚོས་བརྒྱུད་པོ། །རྩ་ལྷར་དོར་ནས་ཚོག་ཤེས་ནོར་
ལྡན་པས། །བརྒྱུད་པ་འདི་ཡི་གདུང་རབས་མི་གཅོད་ན། །སྐྱབ་པའི་
གཙོ་པོ་བླ་མ་སྐྱབ་པ་དང་། །མཆོད་པའི་གཙོ་པོ་བླ་མ་མཆོད་པ་དང་།
།ཆམས་ཤེན་གཙོ་པོ་གསོལ་བ་འདེབས་པ་ལ། །གྱིས་ཤེས་བགའན་
བརྒྱུད་གོང་མའི་གསུངས་པ་ལྟར། །ཁྱེ་གཉིག་སྐྱབ་ལ་འབད་ན་ཅིས་
མི་འཚོད། །མདོ་རྒྱུད་ལུང་དང་གྲུབ་པའི་ཞལ་བཞེས་ལགས།

the merit of accomplishing vast amounts of virtue for as many
eons as there are sands of the River Ganges without this connection. So it is taught extensively in the Buddhist scriptures
and treatises.

In accord with all profound meanings in sutra, tantra, and
    upadeśa,
this is especially exalted over all by the descent of blessings.
If the dull-witted endeavor with intense devotion,
let alone those with faith, diligence, and wisdom,
the ocean of existence will shrink to the water in a footprint.
Since the lineage of genuine realization is unbroken
from Vajradhara down to the root guru,
the power of the root and lineage gurus' blessing suffices.
Therefore the activity of fortunate ones is now.
Since even the seven jewels and the wealth of a ruler
are said to be like a hollow plantain tree, they are bases of
    evil and suffering.
Discard this life's deeds and eight worldly concerns
like roots and gain the wealth of contentment.
In the legacy of this uninterrupted lineage,
the principal practice is the guru practice,
the principal offering is the guru offering,
the principal application is supplication.
So as the previous Kagyü masters said: "Do it!"
If you strive in practice with single focus, why wouldn't you
    thrive?
That is the promise of the sutras, tantras, transmissions, and
    adepts.

།བརྒྱུད་པ་འདི་དང་གདམས་པ་འདི་ཉིད་ལ། །སྤྱན་སྙེས་དང་པས་
ཕྱོགས་ཚམ་མཚོན་པར་བྱས། །ཁྱིས་སྟོའི་དབང་གིས་ནོངས་པའི་
ཚོགས་མ་ལུས། །ཐོག་མེད་ཉེས་སྤྱང་རྣམས་དང་ཆབས་ཅིག་ཏུ། །རྩ་
བ་བརྒྱུད་པའི་དཔལ་ལྡན་བླ་མར་བཤགས། །རྣམ་དཀར་མཆིས་ན་
བདག་གཞན་འབྲེལ་ཐོགས་མཚོན། །མཁའ་མཉམ་ཡིད་ཅན་མ་ལུས་
ཕྱག་རྒྱ་ཆེའི། །གོ་འཕང་རྩོལ་མེད་འཐོབ་པའི་རྒྱུ་གྱུར་ཅིག །ཅེས་པ་
འདི་འང་དུས་འཁོར་ཆུས་ལུགས་དཔལ་རང་བྱུང་ཞབས་ཀྱིས་བཞེད་
པས། བདག་ཅག་གི་སྟོན་པ་ཐུབ་པའི་དབང་པོ་ས་ཁྱི་ལོར་མཛོན་
པར་སངས་རྒྱས་ཏེ་ཚོས་འཁོར་བསྐོར་ནས་བགྲང་བྱ་ཉིས་སྟོང་
བརྒྱད་བརྒྱ་བཅོ་བརྒྱད་པ་ཤིང་ལུག་ས་ག་ཟླ་བའི་དཀར་ཕྱོགས་དགེ་
བར། ཕྱུག་ན་པདྨོ་དཔལ་གཀྲ་ཀ་ཡབ་སྲས་ཀྱི་ཞབས་རྟུལ་སྟི་བོར་
རེག་པའི་བན་རྒན་མ་ཏི་བ་ཊེས་དོན་བསྡུན་རྒྱས་པས་ཀུན་གཟིགས་
བསྟན་པའི་ཉིན་བྱེད་ཀྱི་གསུང་གི་སྲང་བ་ལ་བརྟེན་ནས་སྨྱུང་ཆེན་
དལ་འབབ་ཀྱི་འགྲམ་ཏོགས་ཟོད་གསལ་ཐང་གི་དབེན་པར་གཅིག་
པུར་གནས་སྐབས་རང་གི་བརྗེད་བྱང་དུ་ཤུག་རིས་སུ་བསྒྱུར་བ་དགེ
ཞིགས་འཕེལ། སརྦ་མངྒ་ལོ།། ॥

With spontaneous faith in this lineage and this instruction,
I have gestured in the direction [of its meaning],
but due to my immature intellect, it is full of mistakes.
This, together with all faults and failings since beginningless
        time,
I acknowledge before the glorious root and lineage gurus.
If there is anything good, may it cause myself and others
        connected with it,
and by extension all sentient beings throughout space,
to effortlessly attain the state of mahāmudrā.

According to the date calculations in the *Kālacakra Tantra*,
to which the glorious Venerable Rangjung adhered, from the
time our Teacher Śākyamuni manifested buddhahood in the
earth dog year and turned the wheel of the Dharma, it is calcu-
lated to be 2818. In the virtue of the full moon of the [fourth]
month (*vaiśākha*) of the wood sheep year (1895), touching to
my head the dust beneath the feet of the lotus-holding glorious
succession of Karmapas, this old *maṇi*-mumbling monk composed this as a memorandum to myself based on the teachings
of Kunzik Situ Tenpai Nyinjé's exhaustively-presented definitive meaning, while staying alone in the isolated place of radi-
ant white sand on the banks of a slowly flowing river.

May virtue flourish.

Sarva maṅgalaṃ

Notes

1. Karma Rinchen Dargyé, *Excellent Vase of Elixir* (*Nges don phyag rgya chen po'i smon lam gyi 'grel chung bdud rtsi'i bum bzang*).

2. Gray, "Imprints of the 'Great Seal,'" 425.

3. *Phyag ni ston pa'i ye shes / rgya ni de las mi 'da' bas / chen po gong na med pa'o.* I wrote this down from the retreat master Lama Tenpa so long ago that I have forgotten the source.

4. Situ Tenpai Nyinjé, *Oral Transmission of the Supreme Siddhas*, 68; quoting from Vajrapāṇi, *Instructions from the Successive Guru Lineage*, 179a2.

5. See Dalton, "Mahāmudrā and Samayamudrā in the Dunhuang Documents and Beyond."

6. Roberts, *Mind of Mahāmudrā*, 3. See Roger Jackson's translations of dohās from the original Apabhraṃśa language in *Tantric Treasures*.

7. Dakpo Tashi Namgyal, *Phyag chen zla ba'i 'od zer*, ff.108b–110b.

8. Jamgön Kongtrul, *Treasury of Knowledge, Book 8, Part 4: Esoteric Instructions*, 138–39.

9. *Sdom gsum rab dbye*, translated by Jared Rhoton as *A Clear Differentiation of the Three Codes*.

10. Jamgön Kongtrul, *Treasury of Knowledge, Book 8, Part Four: Esoteric Instructions*, 212.

11. Jared Rhoton put the first documented written reply to a few passages as coming from the fourth Shamar, Chökyi Drakpa (1453–1524), some two and a half centuries later.

12. See for example Gorampa Sönam Sengé, *Complete Explanation of A Clear Differentiation of the Three Codes.*

13. See my research in an unpublished paper, "As for the Blessing of Vajravārāhī, Marpa Lhodrakpa Does Not Have It."

14. Mathes, "Blending the Sūtras with the Tantras," 225.

15. *Sdom gsum rab dbye'i spyi ti ga byed pa bdag thang chad do.* In Padma Karpo, *Pith of Dharma*, 4–5.

16. Roberts, *Mind of Mahāmudrā*, 9.

17. Thanks to Dolma Khyab for his help clarifying this story.

18. Liberation through seeing, hearing, recalling, and touching.

19. *Array of Qualities in Mañjuśrī's Buddha Realm*, 279a. The last line in the Kangyur reads *de 'dre'i 'bras bu thob par 'gyur*, but the meaning is the same.

20. Aśvaghoṣa II, *Gurupañcāśikā*, 10a2–12a2.

21. The six limits and the four modes (*mtha' drug tshul bzhi*), the indispensable keys for unlocking the meaning of the tantras. The six limits are the views of the (1) expedient meaning (*drang don*), (2) definitive meaning (*nges don*), (3) implied (*dgongs pa can*), (4) not implied (*dgongs pa can ma yin pa*), (5) literal (*sgra ji bzhin pa*), and (6) not literal (*sgra ji bzhin ma yin pa*). The four modes

(*tshul bzhi*) are the (1) literal (*tshig*), (2) general (*spyi*), (3) hidden (*sbas*), and the (4) ultimate (*mthar thug*).

22. Nāgārjuna, *In Praise of Dharmadhātu*, verse 17, 64a7.

23. *Sems yid rnam shes*, although *sems* is usually understood as "mind" or "mental consciousness," here, according to Ācārya Lama Tenpa, it refers to the all-ground consciousness.

24. Maitreyanātha, *Mahāyānottaratantraśāstra*, or *Uttaratantraśāstra* 54b1–45a6.

25. Constituent (*khams*; Skt. *dhātu*) in this context is used as a synonym for the essence or potential for being buddha (Skt: *tathāgatagarbha*), commonly referred to as "buddha nature."

26. Nāgārjuna, *In Praise of Dharmadhātu*, verse 11, 64a3. Following the Tengyur edition, the last line should read *nyon mongs 'ba' zhig bskyed par zad* rather than *ngal ba 'ba' zhig skyed par zad* ("effort generates nothing but exhaustion").

27. *Zung 'jug rab tu mi gnas pa'i dbu ma*. Of the seemingly vast classifications of Madhyamaka, there are two schools called "those who logically establish illusion" (*sgyu ma rigs grub pa*) and "proponents of total nonabiding" (*rab tu mi gnas par smra ba*). Jamgön Kongtrul, *The Treasury of Knowledge, Book 6, Part 3: Frameworks of Buddhist Philosophy*, 367–68, n617. A further division into "four kinds of nonabiding" consists of the total nonabiding of emptiness, the total nonabiding of severed continuity, the total nonabiding of equanimity, and the total nonabiding of unity. See Brunnhölzl, *Center of the Sunlit Sky*, all of chapter 3.

28. *Mtha' bral.* A note about this ubiquitous term "free of extremes." Although it indicates so-called extremes of believing in the permanence of objects or a kind of nihilism, it is not just these extremes but virtually any kind of reference point at all, for even a centrist position can be a reference.

29. Not a sutra but a treatise by Jñānagarbha, *Distinguishing the Two Truths*, 2a4–5.

30. A reference to Situ Tenpai Nyinjé's commentary on the same text. See Situ Tenpai Nyinjé, *Oral Transmission of the Supreme Siddhas*, 225–28. Compared to the rest of Situ's commentary, this section *is* rather short.

31. Nāgārjuna, *Root Verses on the Middle Way Called Wisdom*, chap. 24, verse 18, 15a6.

32. *Ḍākinī Vajra Tent Tantra,* chap. 6, 44a4. There, *gang zag* ("persons") replaces *sems can* ("sentient beings"). For context, the last two lines of the verse are: "The abiding meaning of consciousness, or not something external" (*rnam par shes pa'i gnas don nam / phyi rol gyur pa yod ma yin*).

33. Saraha, *Songs of the Dohā Treasury*, 72b5. This particular quotation comes from the dohā known as "The People's Dohā" in Saraha's trilogy of advice to the king, the queen, and the people.

34. Saraha, *Dohā Treasury of Mahāmudrā Instructions*, 123b2.

35. Although here attributed to Nāgārjuna, it is found in Maitreyanātha, *Distinguishing the Middle from the Extremes*, chap. 1, 40b4, with slight variations. It is also quoted in *Kagyü Mahāmudrā Dharma Cycle*, where it is attributed to *Secret Lamp Tantra* (*Gsang ba'i sgron me'i*

rgyud). The full citation reads: "Through relying on the reference points / the nonreferential itself will fully emerge. / When accustomed to the nonreferential, / the essence of the nonreferential is achieved."

36. The gloss here refers to Nāgārjuna's *Suhṛllekha*, 42b6. The passage there has been translated by the Padmakara Translation Group as "Wildness and remorse, and hateful thoughts, / And dullness-somnolence, and yearning lust, / And doubt are hindrances—please know these five / Are thieves that steal the gem of virtuous deeds." See *Nagarjuna's Letter to a Friend*, 108.

37. *'Du byed brgyad.* The eight remedies are aspiration or interest (*mos pa*), exertion (*rtsol ba*), faith (*dad pa*), flexibility (*shin sbyangs*), recollection or mindfulness (*dran pa*), awareness (*shes bzhin*), attention (*sems pa*), and equanimity (*shes bzhin*).

38. *Sems dgu* (*sems zhi bar gnas pa'i thabs dgu*). The nine techniques of mental calm abiding are: mental placement (*sems 'jog pa*), constant placement (*rgyun du 'jog pa*), integrated placement (*glan te 'jog pa*), intensified placement (*nye bar 'jog pa*), control (*'dul ba*), calmness (*zhi ba*), quiescence (*rnam par zhi ba*), one-pointedness (*rtse gcig*), and equipoise (*mnyam par 'jog pa*). See Jamgön Kongtrul, *Treasury of Knowledge, Book 6, Parts 1 and 2: Indo-Tibetan Classical Learning and Buddhist Phenomenology*, 428–29.

39. *Zhi byed* (*zhijé*) or the longer name *Sdug bsngal zhi byed* ("Pacification of Suffering") is a general name for the extensive corpus of instructions attributed to the Indian adept called Dampa Sangyé (or Kamalaśrī/Kamālaśīla), and also the name of his lineage or school. See Jamgön

Kongtrul, *Treasury of Precious Instructions, Volume 13: Zhije*.

40. *Gcod* (*chöd*) means to sever, cut, or determine, and refers to the widespread practice developed by the Tibetan yoginī Machik Lapdrön. However, the line here is open to some interpretation; given the long list of named practices in this passage, I regard it as a reference to the Chöd practice of "cutting" negative forces. Another version by Peter Alan Roberts reads "It was taught that even obstacles / from demons, māras, and so on should be exalted." Roberts, *Mahāmudrā and Related Instructions*, 252.

41. From Pakmo Drupa, *Applied Coemergence*, 258–59. This is part of an explanation of the term *lhan cig skyes sbyor* (Skt. *sahaja* or *sahajayoga*), sometimes translated as "connate union." The reproduction here seems to have left important lines out, so I have added the lines missing from there. There are also two important differences: "instructions on valid cognition" (*tshad mai'i gdams ngag*) rather than "guru's instruction" and "joined as/in mind by instructions" (*gdams pas sems su sbyor*) rather than "joined as one." Also Pakmo Drupa attributes this as being "from the mouth of the Lord," presumably his guru Gampopa Sönam Rinchen.

42. Unknown reference. Possibly Rāga Asya, also known as Karma Chakmé.

43. Advayavajra, *Scriptural Commentary on the Songs of the Dohā Treasury*, 198b5.

44. *Rtags bcu.* The ten signs of lucid clarity are: smoke, mirage, clouds, fireflies, sun, moon, shining jewels,

eclipse, stars, and light rays. Roberts, *Mahāmudrā and Related Instructions*, 639, n223.

45. This has not been located in a sutra, but is quoted in many sources, such as Gampopa's *Jewel Ornament of Liberation*, 40b4.

46. Nāgārjuna, *Commentary on Awakening Mind*, verse 2, 41a3.

47. The quotation appears in several places in Gampopa's *Collected Works*, such as *Garland of Pearls*, 12a.

48. Nāgārjuna, *Commentary on Awakening Mind*, 41b3.

49. *Bhu su ku*, or *bu su ku*, an Indian word referring to ordinary daily functions, specifically eating (*bha*), sleeping (*su*), and walking (*ku*). In other words, the yogic conduct of practicing nothing but the basics.

50. This is missing from Mendong Tsampa's commentary and has been added from Situ Tenpai Nyinjé, *Oral Transmission of the Supreme Siddhas*: *bzhi pa sngon gnas rjes dran gyi mngon shes / sems can thams cad kyi so so'i 'das pa dang ma 'ongs pa'i skye ba brgyud mar shes pa.*

51. Maitreyanātha, *Ornament of the Mahāyāna Sutras*, 40b1–45a6.

52. *Āryabhadracaryāpraṇidhānarāja*, 264b2–3 and 264b7. Also known as *Prayer of Excellent Conduct*, this immensely popular prayer is based on a passage in the final part of the *Avataṃsaka Sūtra*. It stands on its own in the *dhāraṇī* section of the Kangyur.

53. The first three of the five treatises (*Byams chos lnga*) composed by Asaṅga and attributed to Maitreya: *Ornament of Clear Realization, Ornament of the Mahāyāna Sutras, Mahāyāna Highest Continuum, Distinguishing Dharma*

from Dharmatā, and *Distinguishing the Middle from the Extremes.*

54. *Bde ba can kyi smon lam* or *Chags med bde smon*, Karma Chakmé's famous prayer based on the Sukhāvatī Sutras. Mendong Tsampa himself composed a commentary to this prayer called *Swift Travel to the Pure Realm: A Short Commentary on the Aspiration Prayer of the Realm of Bliss*, 308–402.

55. *Phyag rgya chen po tshig bsdus* (*Mahāmudrāsañcamitha*). Not in the Tengyur. The two-folia text by this name is in Jamgön Kongtrul, *Treasury of Precious Instructions* (vol. 7, 47–48), and does not mention the four yogas.

56. *Trilogy of Bodhisattva Commentaries.*

57. *Sbyor drug* (Skt. *ṣaḍaṅgayoga*), the six-branch yoga in the tradition of the *Kālacakra Tantra.*

58. According to the *Fortunate Eon Sutra*, one thousand buddhas will appear in this eon. Śākyamuni was the fourth, Maitreya the fifth, and the sixth will be Siṁha (Seng ge, "Lion"). This will be the successor currently known as Karmapa.

59. From Mikyö Dorjé, *Collection of Advice on Mahāmudrā.* There, it begins with "conceptual thoughts as dhar-makāya and appearances as one's own mind, in this Dharma system" (*rnam rtog chos kyi sku dang snang ba rang gi sems zhes*).

60. Although attributed here to Nāgārjuna, and specifically to *Precious Garland [A Letter to the King]* by Tai Situ Tenpai Nyinjé, it is actually found in Āryadeva, *Four Hundred Verse Treatise*, 9a7. Apparently a different translation was used here.

Bibliography

Kangyur (Canonical Scriptures)

Array of Qualities in Mañjuśrī's Buddha Realm. Mañjuśrībuddhakṣetraguṇavyūha. 'Jam dpal gyi sangs rgyas kyi zhing gi yon tan bkod pa. Toh 59, dkon brtsegs, *ga*, 248b1–297a3.

Ḍākinī Vajra Tent Tantra. Ḍākinīvajrapañjarātantra. Mka' 'gro ma rdo rje gur zhes bya ba'i rgyud kyi rgyal po chen po'i brtag pa. Toh 419, rgyud, *nga*, 30a4–65b7.

Fortunate Eon Sutra. Bhadrakalpikasūtra. Bskal pa bzang po'i mdo. Toh 94, mdo sde, *ka*, 1b1–340a5.

Prayer of Samantabhadra's Conduct. Āryabhadracaryāpraṇidhānarāja. 'Phags pa bzang po spyod pa'i smon lam gyi rgyal po. Toh 1095, gzung 'dus, *wam*, 262b3–266a3.

Tengyur (Canonical Treatises)

Advayavajra (Gnyis su med pa'i rdo rje). *Scriptural Commentary on the Songs of the Dohā Treasury. Dohākoṣapañjikā.* Do ha mdzod kyi dka' 'grel. Toh 2256, rgyud, *wi*, 180b3–207a7.

Āryadeva. *The Four Hundred Verse Treatise. Catuḥśataka-śāstra. Bstan bcos bzhi brgya pa zhes bya ba'i tshig le'ur byas pa.* Toh 3846, dbu ma, *tsha,* 1a1–18a7.

Aśvaghoṣa II (Rta dbyangs, 10th century). *Fifty Verses of Guru Devotion. Gurupañcāśikā. Bla ma lnga bcu pa.* Toh 3721, rgyud, *tshu,* 10a2–12a2.

Jñānagarbha. *Distinguishing the Two Truths. Satyadva-yavibhaṅgakārikā. Bden pa gnyis rnam par 'byed pa'i tshig le'ur byas pa.* Toh 3881, dbu ma, *sa,* 1b–3b.

Maitreyanātha. *Distinguishing Dharma from Dharmatā. Dharmadharmatāvibhāga. Chos dang chos nyid rnam par 'byed pa.* Toh 4022, sems tsam, *phi,* 46b–49a.

———.*Distinguishing the Middle from the Extremes. Madh-yāntavibhāga. Dbus dang mtha' rnam par 'byed pa'i tshig le'u byas pa.* Toh 4021, sems tsam, *phi,* 40b1–45a6.

———. *Mahāyāna Highest Continuum. Ratnagotravibhāga Mahāyānottaratantraśāstra. Theg pa chen po rgyud bla ma'i bstan bcos.* Toh 4024, sems tsam, *phi,* 54b1–45a6.

———. *Ornament of Clear Realization. Abhisamayālaṃkāra. Mngon par rtogs pa'i rgyan.* Toh 3786, shes phyin, *ka,* 1b–13a.

———. *Ornament of the Mahāyāna Sutras. Mahāyā-nosūtrālaṃkāra. Mdo sde brgyan.* Toh 4020, sems tsam, *phi,* 1a1–39a4.

Nāgārjuna. *Commentary on Awakening Mind. Bodhicitta-vivaraṇa. Byang chub sems 'grel.* Toh 1800, rgyud, *ngi,* 41a1–42b5.

———. *Letter to a Friend. Suhṛllekha. Bshes pa'i spring yig.* Toh 4182, spring yig, *nge,* 40b4–46b3.

———. *In Praise of Dharmadhātu. Dharmadhātustava. Chos kyi byings su bstod pa.* Toh 1118, bstod tshogs, *ka,* 63b5–67b3.

———. *Root Verses on the Middle Way Called Wisdom*. *Pra-jñānāmamūlamadhyamakakārikā*. *Dbu ma rtsa ba'i thsig le'ur byas pa shes rab ces bya ba*. Toh 3824, dbu ma, *tsa*, 1a1–19a6.

Saraha. *Dohā Treasury of Mahāmudrā Instructions*. *Dohākoṣanāma mahāmudropadeśa*. *Do ha mdzod ces bya ba phyag rgya chen po'i man ngag*. Toh 2273, rgyud, *zhi*, 122a3–124a7.

———. *Songs of the Dohā Treasury*. *Dohākoṣagīti*. *Do ha mdzod kyi glu*. Toh 2224, rgyud, *wi*, 70b5–77a3.

Trilogy of Bodhisattva Commentaries. *Sems 'grel skor gsum*. One each by Puṇḍarīka, Vajragarbha, and Vajrapāṇi, focusing on the *Kālacakra*, *Hevajra*, and *Cakrasaṃvara* tantras, respectively. Toh 1347, 1180, and 1402.

Vajrapāṇi. *Instructions from the Successive Guru Lineage*. *Guruparamparakramapadeśa*. *Bla ma brgyud pa'i rim pa'i man ngag*. Toh 3716, rgyud, *tsu*, 164b2–183a5.

Tibetan Works

Bokar Tulku, Karma Ngedön Chökyi Lodrö ('Bo dkar sprul sku Karma nges don chos kyi blo gros). *Lamp for the Minds of the Faithful: A Rough Sketch of the Activities of the Glorious Guru*. *Dpal ldan bla ma'i mdzad rnam rag bsdus mos ldan yid kyi sgron me*. In *Collected Works of Mendong Tsampa Rinpoché*, vol. 3, 490–500.

Collected Works of Mendong Tsampa Rinpoché, Karma Ngedön Tengyé. 3 vols. Reproduced from tracings from the collected block prints impressed from the xylographs preserved at Sman Dgon Thub-chen-bde-chen-gling. Bir, HP: D. Tsondu Senghe, 1975.

Dakpo Tashi Namgyal (Dwags po Bkra shis rnam rgyal). *Moon-beams of Mahāmudrā. Phyag chen zla ba'i 'od zer.* Tibetan xylograph edition. Sikkim: Rumtek Monastery, n.d.

Gampopa Sönam Rinchen (Gam po pa Bsod nams rin chen). *Collected Works of Gampopa Sönam Rinchen.* 4 vols. Kathmandu: Khenpo S. Tenzin and Lama T. Namgyal, 2000. BDRC W23439.

———. *Garland of Pearls: A Teaching for the Assembly. Tshogs chos mu tig gi phreng ba.* In *Collected Works of Gampopa Sönam Rinchen,* vol. 1, 577–669.

———. *Jewel Ornament of Liberation. Dam chos yid bzhin nor bu thar pa rin po che'i rgyan.* In *Collected Works of Gampopa Sönam Rinchen,* vol. 4, 193–660.

Gorampa Sönam Sengé (Go ram pa Bsod nams seng ge). *Complete Explanation of A Clear Differentiation of the Three Codes, Clarifying the Intention of the Victor's Speech. Sdom pa gsum gyi rab tu dbye ba'i rnam bshad rgyal ba'i gsung rab kyi dgong pa gsal ba.* In *The Collected Works of Kun-mkyen Go-rams-pa bsod-nams-seng-ge,* vol. 9. Dehra Dun: Sakya College, 1979. BDRC W11249-0439.

Kagyü Mahāmudrā Dharma Cycle. Bka' brgyud pa'i phyag chen chos skor. Swayambhu, Kathmandu: Karma Lekshey Ling, 2012. BDRC W3JT13326.

Karma Rinchen Dargyé (Karma Rin chen dar rgyas). *Excellent Vase of Elixir: Short Commentary on the Aspiration Prayer of Definitive Mahāmudrā. Nges don phyag rgya chen po'i smon lam gyi 'grel chung bdud rtsi'i bum bzang.* Swayambu, Kathmandu: Karma Lekshey Ling, 2012. BDRC W3JT13321.

Mendong Tsampa, Karma Ngedön Tengyé (Sman sdong mtshams pa, Karma nges don bstan rgyas). *Collected Works of Mendong Tsampa Rinpoché.* 3 vols. Bir, HP: D. Tsondu Senghe, 1975.

———. *Ornament of Dakpo Kagyü Thought: A Short Commentary on the Mahāmudrā Aspiration Prayer. Phyag chen smon lam 'grel chung dwags brgyud dgongs rgyan.* In *Collected Works of Mendong Tsampa Rinpoché,* vol. 1, 403–74.

———. *Swift Travel to the Pure Realm: A Short Commentary on the Aspiration Prayer of the Realm of Bliss. Bde smon 'grel chung zhing khams myur bgrod.* In *Collected Works of Mendong Tsampa Rinpoché,* vol. 1, 308–402.

Mikyö Dorjé (Mi bskyod rdo rje), the eighth Karmapa. *Collection of Advice on Mahāmudrā. Phyag rgya chen po sgros 'bum.* In *Collected Works of Karma pa Mi bskyod rdo rje,* vol. 24, 3–468. Lhasa, 2004. BDRC W8039.

Nāropa. *Concise Words on Mahāmudrā. *Mahāmudrāsañcamitha. Phyag rgya chen po tshig bsdus.* Included in Jamgön Kongtrul's compiled *Treasury of Precious Instructions,* vol. 7, 47–48. (Not in the Tengyur.)

Pakmo Drupa (Phag mo gru pa). *Applied Coemergence. Lhan cig skyes sbyor.* In *Collected Works of Pakmo Drupa,* vol. *nga* (4), 256–82. Kathmandu: Khenpo S. Tenzin and Lama T. Namgyal, 2003.

Padma Karpo (Padma dkar po). *The Pith of Dharma: Complete Explanation of the Bodiless Ḍākinī. Lus med mkha' 'gro'i chos sde'i rnam par bshad pa chos kyi nying khu.* In *Collected Works of Kun mkhyen Padma dkar po.* Darjeeling: Kargyud Sungrab Nyamso Khang, 1973–74. BDRC W10736.

Rāga Asya [Karma Chakmé]. *Aspiration Prayer for the Realm of Bliss. Chags med bde smon/ Rnam dag bde chen zhing gi smon lam mkhas grub rā ga a syas mdzad pa.* Boudanath, Nepal: Nyag rong lha rje rgyal sras 'jam dbyangs bstan 'dzin, 1932. BDRC W3CN1604

Situ Tenpai Nyinjé (Si tu Bstan pa'i nyin byed). *Oral Transmission of the Supreme Siddhas: A Commentary on the Prayer of the Definitive Mahāmudrā. Nges don phyag rgya chen po'i smon lam gyi 'grel pa grub mchog gi zhal lung.* In *Collected Works of Chökyi Jungné (Gsung 'bum of Chos kyi 'byung gnas),* vol. 8. Sansal, Kangra Dist., HP: Palpung sungrab nyamso khang: 1990. BDRC W26630.

Translator's Bibliography

Brunnhölzl, Karl. *The Center of the Sunlit Sky: Madhyamaka in the Kagyü Tradition.* Nitartha Institute Series. Ithaca, NY: Snow Lion, 2007.

Callahan, Elizabeth M., trans. *Moonbeams of Mahāmudrā,* by Dakpo Tashi Namgyal; With *Dispelling the Darkness of Ignorance* by Wangchuk Dorje, the Ninth Karmapa. The Tsadra Foundation Series. Boulder, CO: Snow Lion, 2019.

Dalton, Jacob P. "*Mahāmudrā* and *Samayamudrā* in the Dunhuang Documents and Beyond." In Jackson and Mathes, *Mahāmudrā in India and Tibet,* 123–41.

Dorje, Lama Sherab, trans. *The Eighth Situpa on the Third Karmapa's Mahamudra Prayer.* Boulder, CO: Snow Lion, 1995 and 2004.

Gray, David B. "Imprints of the 'Great Seal': On the expand-
    ing semantic range of the term *mudrā* in eighth through
    eleventh century Indian Buddhist literature." *JIABS* 34,
    nos. 1–2 (2011): 421–81.

Harding, Sarah. "As for the Blessing of Vajravārāhī, Marpa
    Lhodrakpa does not have it." Unpublished, Tsadra Foun-
    dation Blog, March 25, 2011.

Jackson, Roger R. *Tantric Treasures: Three Collections of Mys-
    tical Verse from Buddhist India*. Oxford: Oxford Univer-
    sity Press, 2004.

Jackson, Roger R., and Klaus-Dieter Mathes, eds. *Mahāmudrā
    in India and Tibet*. Brill's Tibetan Studies Library 44.
    Leiden: Brill, 2019.

Jamgön Kongtrul Lodrö Tayé. *The Treasury of Knowledge,
    Book 6, Parts 1 and 2: Indo-Tibetan Classical Learning and
    Buddhist Phenomenology*. Translated by the Kalu Rin-
    poché Translation Group (Gyurme Dorje). Boston: Snow
    Lion, 2012.

———. *The Treasury of Knowledge, Book 6, Part 3: Frameworks
    of Buddhist Philosophy*. Translated by the Kalu Rinpoché
    Translation Group (Elizabeth M. Callahan). Ithaca, NY:
    Snow Lion, 2007.

———. *The Treasury of Knowledge, Book 8, Part 4: Esoteric
    Instructions*. Translated by the Kalu Rinpoché Translation
    Group (Sarah Harding). Ithaca, NY: Snow Lion, 2007.

———, comp. *The Treasury of Precious Instructions: Essential
    Teachings of the Eight Practice Lineages of Tibet, Volume 13:
    Zhije*. Translated by Sarah Harding. Boulder, CO: Snow
    Lion, 2019.

Mathes, Klaus-Dieter. "Blending the Sūtras with the Tantras: The Influence of Maitrīpa and His Circle on the Formation of *Sūtra Mahāmudrā* in the Kagyu Schools." In *Tibetan Buddhist Literature and Praxis: Studies in Its Formative Period, 900–1400: Proceedings of the Tenth Seminar of the International Association for Tibetan Studies*, edited by Ronald M. Davidson and Christian K. Wedemeyer, 201–27. Leiden: Brill, 2006.

———. "Can Sūtra Mahāmudrā be Justified on the Basis of Maitrīpa's Apratiṣṭhānavāda?" In *Pramāṇakīrtiḥ: Papers Dedicated to Ernst Steinkellner on the Occasion of His 70th Birthday*, edited by B. Kellner, H. Lasic, M. T. Much, H. Tauscher, 545–66. Wiener Studien zur Tibetologie und Buddhismuskunde 70, no. 2. Vienna: Arbeitskreis für tibetische und buddhistische Studien, 2007.

Nagarjuna's Letter to a Friend: With Commentary by Kangyur Rinpoche. Translated by the Padmakara Translation Group. Ithaca, NY: Snow Lion, 2005.

Tai Situ Rinpoche, XII Khentin. *The Third Karmapa's Mahāmudrā Prayer*. Translated by Rosemarie Fuchs. Ithaca, NY: Snow Lion, 2002.

Rhoton, Jared Douglas. *A Clear Differentiation of the Three Codes: Essential Distinctions among the Individual Liberation, Great Vehicle, and Tantric Systems*. Albany: State University of New York Press, 2002.

Rangjung Dorje, the Third Karmapa. *The Profound Inner Principles* with Jamgön Kongtrul Lodrö Taye's Commentary, *"Illuminating 'The Profound Principles.'"* Translated by Elizabeth M. Callahan. Boston: Snow Lion, 2014.

Roberts, Peter Alan, trans. *Mahāmudrā and Related Instruc-tions: Core Teachings of the Kagyü Schools.* Boston: Wis-dom Publications, 2011.

———. *The Mind of Mahāmudrā.* Boston: Wisdom Publica-tions, 2014.

Situ Tenpai Nyinjé. "Oral Transmission of the Supreme Sid-dhas: A Commentary on Prayer for the Definitive Mean-ing, the Mahāmudrā." In Roberts, *Mahāmudrā and Related Instructions*, 175–288.

INDEX

ABOUT THE TRANSLATOR

SARAH HARDING has been studying and practicing Buddhism since
1974, and has been teaching and
translating since completing a
three-year retreat in 1980 under the
guidance of Kyabjé Kalu Rinpoché.
She was a professor at Naropa University for twenty-five years, in
Boulder, Colorado, where she cur-
rently resides, and has been a fellow of the Tsadra Foundation
since 2000. She specializes in literature with a focus on tantric
practice. Her publications include *Creation and Completion:
Essential Points of Tantric Meditation*; *The Treasury of Knowledge: Esoteric Instructions*; *Niguma, Lady of Illusion*; and four
volumes on Chöd, Zhijé, and Shangpa Kagyü from the *Treasury of Precious Instructions*.

What to Read Next
from Wisdom Publications

Creation and Completion
Essential Points of Tantric Meditation
Jamgön Kongtrul
Translated by Sarah Harding

"Creation and completion meditation is the cornerstone of tantric Buddhist practice, and draws upon a rich array of techniques and presumptions relating to moral culitvation. This book will be of great interest to both scholars and practitioners of Tibetan Buddhism."—Janet Gyatso, Hershey Chair of Buddhist Studies, Harvard University

Four Tibetan Lineages
Core Teachings of Pacification, Severance, Shangpa Kagyü, and Bodongpa
Translated by Sarah Harding

Drawing primarily from the Pacification, Severance, Shangpa Kagyü, and Bodongpa traditions, *Four Tibetan Lineages* presents some of Tibet's most transformative yet lesser-known teachings on meditative practice.

Ornament of Precious Liberation
By Gampopa
Translated by Ken Holmes
Foreword by His Holiness the Karmapa

"This text has the power of a direct transmission from master to student . . . Though there are several earlier translations of *Ornament of Precious Liberation*, this translation is the most readable and faithful."—His Holiness the Karmapa, Ogyen Trinley Dorje

Mahāmudrā and Related Instructions
Core Teachings of the Kagyü Schools
Translated by Peter Alan Roberts

"This collection is a treasury of 'great seal' teachings from the most renowned gurus of the Mahāmudrā lineage, each text precious beyond compare. Every page exudes freshness of realization, holding the keys to our own personal awakening."—Judith Simmer-Brown, Naropa University, author of *Dakini's Warm Breath*

Sounds of Innate Freedom
The Indian Texts of Mahāmudrā
Translated and introduced by Karl Brunnhölzl

This collection offers a brilliant window into the richness of the vast ocean of Indian mahāmudrā texts cherished in all Tibetan lineages, particularly in the Kagyü tradition, giving us a clear view of the sources of one of the world's great contemplative traditions.

About Wisdom Publications

Wisdom Publications is the leading publisher of classic and contemporary Buddhist books and practical works on mindfulness. To learn more about us or to explore our other books, please visit our website at wisdomexperience.org or contact us at the address below.

Wisdom Publications
199 Elm Street
Somerville, MA 02144 USA

We are a 501(c)(3) organization, and donations in support of our mission are tax deductible.

Wisdom Publications is affiliated with the Foundation for the Preservation of the Mahayana Tradition (FPMT).